Whitman THE OFFICIAL RED BOOK®

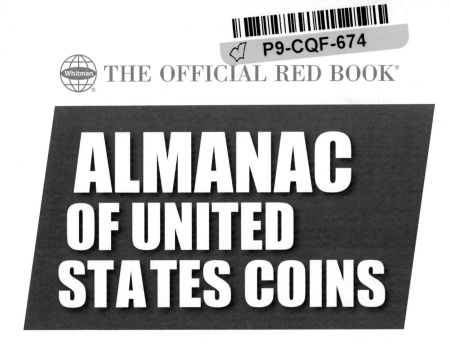

ALMANAC OF UNITED STATES COINS

FIRST EDITION
2013

Edited by
Dennis B. Tucker,
Whitman Publishing, LLC

An Illustrated Catalog of Useful and Entertaining Information

With DETAILED PHOTOGRAPHS to Identify Your Coins

And RETAIL PRICE CHARTS Telling How Much They're Worth

Plus INSIDER TIPS on Treasures Waiting to be Discovered in Your Pocket Change

Based on the EXPERTISE of More than 100 Professional Coin Dealers and Researchers

Also Featuring Amusing Stories, Amazing Essays, and Astounding Facts and Figures About All Manner of Rare and Historical Coins of the United States of America

THE OFFICIAL RED BOOK™
ALMANAC OF UNITED STATES COINS

THE OFFICIAL RED BOOK and THE OFFICIAL RED BOOK OF
UNITED STATES COINS are trademarks of Whitman Publishing, LLC.

www.whitman.com

0794839258
Printed in the United States of America.

© 2013 Whitman Publishing, LLC
3101 Clairmont Road · Suite G · Atlanta GA 30329

For a complete listing of numismatic reference books, supplies,
and storage products, visit us at www.Whitman.com.

Scan this QR code to browse
Whitman Publishing's full
catalog of coin-related books,
supplies, storage and
display products.

CONTENTS

1: An Introduction to U.S. Coins 1

2: Today's Rare-Coin Market. 7

3: How to Grade Your Coins 13

4: Proof Coins 20

5: Third-Party Grading and Authentication 22

6: Collecting Colonial and Early American Coins. 24

7: Half Cents and Large Cents. 27

8: Small Cents 35

9: Two-Cent Pieces. 53

10: Three-Cent Pieces 56

11: Nickel Five-Cent Pieces 62

12: Half Dimes 75

13: Dimes. 78

14: Twenty-Cent Coins 89

15: Quarter Dollars. 92

16: Half Dollars. 107

17: Silver Dollars. 121

18: Gold Coins 146

19: Commemorative Coins. 154

20: Proof and Mint Sets 161

21: Silver, Gold, and Platinum Bullion 168

22: Tokens and Medals. 173

23: United States / Philippines Coins 176

24: Misstrikes and Error Coins. 181

Appendix A: Bullion Values of Silver and Gold Coins 184

Appendix B: Famous Coin Hoards and Treasures 186

CONTRIBUTORS AND CREDITS

Coin values in the *Almanac of United States Coins* are derived from data submitted by these contributors to the annually issued *Guide Book of United States Coins* (the hobby's best-selling "Red Book"). Each is a recognized expert in U.S. coins and a longtime professional coin dealer.

Gary Adkins
John Albanese
Mark Albarian
Dominic Albert
Buddy Alleva
Richard S. Appel
Richard M. August
Mitchell A. Battino
Lee J. Bellisario
Mark Borckardt
Q. David Bowers
Kenneth Bressett
Philip Bressett
Larry Briggs
H. Robert Campbell
J.H. Cline
Elizabeth Coggan
Alan Cohen
Gary Cohen
Stephen M. Cohen
Steve Contursi
Adam Crum
Raymond Czahor
Sheridan Downey
Steven Ellsworth
Mike Fuljenz
Chuck Furjanic
Jeff Garrett
Dennis M. Gillio
Ronald J. Gillio
Ira M. Goldberg

Lawrence Goldberg
Kenneth M. Goldman
J.R. Grellman
Tom Hallenbeck
James Halperin
Ash Harrison
Steven Hayden
Brian Hendelson
Gene L. Henry
John W. Highfill
Jesse Iskowitz
Steve Ivy
James J. Jelinski
Larry Johnson
Donald H. Kagin
Bradley S. Karoleff
Jim Koenings
Richard A. Lecce
Julian M. Leidman
Stuart Levine
Kevin Lipton
Denis W. Loring
David McCarthy
Chris McCawley
Robert T. McIntire
Harry Miller
Lee S. Minshull
Scott P. Mitchell
Michael C. Moline
Paul Montgomery
Casey Noxon

Paul Nugget
Mike Orlando
John M. Pack
Joseph Parrella
Robert M. Paul
William P. Paul
Joel Rettew Jr.
Joel Rettew Sr.
Robert Rhue
Greg Rohan
Maurice Rosen
Gerald R. Scherer Jr.
Cherie Schoeps
Richard J. Schwary
Roger Siboni
James Simek
Craig Smith
Rick Snow
David M. Sundman
Anthony J. Swiatek
Anthony Terranova
Troy Thoreson
Ben Todd
Jerry Treglia
Frank Van Valen
Fred Weinberg
Douglas Winter
David Wnuck
Mark S. Yaffe

Special image credits are due to the Library of Congress, the Smithsonian Institution, Stack's Bowers Galleries, the United States Mint, and the Whitman Coin & Collectibles Expo.

1

AN INTRODUCTION TO UNITED STATES COINS

Money—it makes the world go 'round.

Today we think of money as coins, paper currency, and electronic debit. Back in colonial times, starting in the early 1600s, Americans used all kinds of things as money, including beaver skins, strings of wampum (periwinkle, quahog, and other shells fashioned into beads), plugs of tobacco, quantities of salt, and iron nails. This was because coins—whether gold, silver, or copper—didn't stay in the colonies very long. The colonists had to use them to pay British and other European merchants for products they needed to stay alive and prosper in the New World.

Amongst themselves, the colonists rarely paid with coins or paper currency. Barter, or "country pay," was common—a farmer would trade some of his vegetables for pots and pans, a shoemaker would exchange boots for fresh eggs and salted pork.

The European settlers also traded with Native Americans, who supplied them with animal skins, food, and other goods that the colonists could either use themselves or ship from New England to the mother country, Great Britain.

The wealthy British had a taste for New World commodities like furs (all the rage in fashionable circles), tobacco for smoking, fish and meat for their dinner tables, and sugar from the warmer regions. British industry used American lumber, cloth, and raw metal to create useful and/or decorative finished products—things the colonists couldn't make themselves because they lacked an industrial base. The Americans had to buy from England most of their machinery, hardware, weapons, fine furniture, and other "high-tech" products.

The British government didn't allow the colonists to mint their own coins (this prohibition made it easier for the Empire to control overseas trade). When cash *was* available for transactions, pretty much any coin, from any country, would do. The most popular were British guineas, French louis, German thalers, Dutch ducats, and various Spanish coins, including gold doubloons and, particularly, the Spanish milled dollar, or piece of eight.

Over time the colonies became more settled and their commerce expanded. Bartering for chickens and paying with tobacco only went so far—the colonists felt a growing need for cold, hard cash. Starting in the mid-1600s various local governments, private citizens, and businesses struck coins and tokens to fill that need. (See the chapter on "Collecting Colonial and Early American Coins.") Most of these issues were copper; some were silver, and a few gold. Some of these coins were authorized by British royal order, but most were made in secret because striking coinage was still a right reserved by the Crown.

After the colonies declared their independence from Britain, Americans granted their states the right to coin money, with Congress regulating. New Hampshire, Massachusetts, Connecticut, New York, New Jersey, and Vermont each struck their own state coinage in the late 1700s. On the national level, Congress resolved on March 3, 1791, that a mint should be established, and authorized President George Washington to hire enough artists and buy the

The New World's colonists bartered amongst themselves, and also traded with Native Americans. Coins were not a common sight in their day-to-day transactions. (This illustration from the magazine *Puck*, 1913, lampoons the popular concept of early settlers bargaining with the Indians using trinkets and brightly colored cloth.)

machinery needed to make coins. A few months later, in his third annual message to Congress (October 1791), Washington strongly recommended the immediate creation of a national mint. Finally, by the Act of April 2, 1792, a mint was authorized. Within a few months construction began on its buildings, in Philadelphia (the capital city). Copper cents and half cents were struck the following year, with silver and gold coins not far behind.

Since that time the U.S. Mint has struck billions of coins, of hundreds of different designs and many different metals, sizes, and denominations. Today, collecting those coins is a popular hobby enjoyed by millions of Americans. *The Official RED BOOK® Almanac of United States Coins* is your entry-level guide to this rewarding pastime.

The Spanish piece of eight—a silver coin worth eight reales—was a standard money unit in America from the early 1700s through the end of the colonial period and beyond. These coins were known as *milled dollars,* because of their "milled" or patterned edges, or as *Pillar dollars,* because of the two Pillars of Hercules shown on one side.

This time-honored coin was part of the famous "pirate treasures" of romantic fiction (and historical fact). The Spanish government minted millions of coins from the silver mined in its Mexican and Central and South American colonies. The milled dollar and its fractional parts (one-half, one, two, and four reales) were the most common of coins used by American settlers, even in the British colonies. Sometimes they would cut a coin into pieces to make small change.

The milled dollar was so widespread that Thomas Jefferson, on September 2, 1776, recommended to the Continental Congress that the new nation should adopt it as its monetary unit of value. This didn't happen, but even after the Revolutionary War ended (in 1783), and after the U.S. Mint was established (in 1792), the Spanish dollar and its parts continued to circulate in the United States with official sanction, up until the late 1850s.

One real equaled 12-1/2 cents and was known as a *bit.* A quarter of a dollar thus became known as *two bits,* a term still understood to mean 25 cents.

The New World's population increased through the 1600s and 1700s, and its businesses, farms, and estates expanded. Americans outgrew their early barter economy and, to keep up with the demands of commerce, felt pressure to mint their own coins—first in the colonies, then (after independence) in the individual states, and then as a sovereign nation.

Coin collecting has been called the "Hobby of Kings," but it's also popular with millions of everyday Americans who love the richness of our nation's history, the artistry of our coinage designs, and the excitement of a good treasure hunt.

2
TODAY'S RARE-COIN MARKET

You can have fun collecting coins without ever walking into a hobby shop or going to a show—there are plenty of interesting (and even uncommon and valuable) coins to be found in everyday pocket change. As your collection grows, though, chances are the "collecting bug" will bite you, and you'll be tempted by older, rarer, and more diverse coins. Don't fight the temptation! Collecting and

Mrs. Edness Wilkens, secretary to Nellie Tayloe Ross, director of the U.S. Mint. An April 1938 publicity release noted that Mrs. Wilkens "for the last four years has been collecting coins as a hobby, thru gifts, trades, and buys," and "she has a collection of over 400 coins ramping from half pennies to the old silver cartwheels [dollar coins]." Being the Mint director's secretary gave Wilkens access to coins that most of us will never see in person (unless they're on display in a coin-show exhibit)—here she's inspecting a 1792 half disme (yes, *disme*), one of the first coins struck at the Philadelphia Mint. Legend has it that the silver for these coins came from Martha Washington's tableware; at that time she and the president lived a short walk down from the Mint, and they are said to have given some of their personal silverware for the nation's first coinage. Today a 1792 half disme, depending on its grade, can be worth anywhere from $8,500 to $325,000—or more. Check Grandpa's old cigar box! (coin shown 2x actual size)

investing in rare coins can be a rewarding experience if you approach the calling armed with the right attitude and background knowledge.

Of course, it can just as easily bring costly mistakes if you try to profit from coins without giving serious thought to this unique market.

The best advice for investing in rare coins is to *use common sense*. Would you expect to buy a genuine gold-and-diamond luxury watch from a street vendor for $50? Or to find a unique oil-painting masterpiece at a garage sale? Of course not. The situation is the same with rare coins. For expensive purchases, you

should find a qualified dealer and make an educated evaluation—this increases your chance of making a profitable investment. On the Internet, visit the sites of the Professional Numismatists Guild (the leading nationwide association of rare-coin dealers, at PNGdealers.com). Many of these dealers have web sites or issue catalogs. Review them and you'll find a great deal of basic, useful information.

At any given time there are many advertisements, infomercials with self-identified experts, and the like—on television, in magazines, and elsewhere—stating that investment in gold, silver, rare coins, and related items is the best way to preserve and increase wealth. Some of these promotions are by firms that aren't part of the established professional numismatic community. Whether you're collecting or investing, you should investigate the background of a potential seller before you make any significant purchases.

Take your time and go slowly. As with paintings and sculptures, securities, and other investments, you can buy coins instantly, but selling them at a profit might be another thing entirely.

Now, don't take these warnings the wrong way. If you're a careful buyer, you can collect and invest successfully—your opportunities today are as great as they were at any time in the past. Inexperienced buyers can purchase coins that have been graded and authenticated by top-rated third-party services to assure their quality (see "Third-Party Grading and Authentication"). There is also more information, in print and online, available for beginners today than ever before. And the pricing of rare coins is very competitive in today's widespread market.

GRADING AND VALUE

The shift in emphasis from collecting to investing on the part of many buyers in recent decades has created a dynamic market and demand for coins. Two side effects are stricter grading methods, and pricing geared to the perceived rarity of coins in various levels of Mint State or Proof perfection. Coins in high grades that have been certified (professionally graded and guaranteed to be authentic) and "slabbed" (encapsulated) may be valued significantly higher than similar coins that are "raw" (not certified and encapsulated).

To learn more about these aspects of the marketplace, see "How to Grade Your Coins" and "Third-Party Grading and Authentication."

For hundreds of years, rare coins and precious metals have been an excellent hedge against inflation and a source of ready money in times of crisis (as long as they were purchased carefully). There is little reason to think this will change in the future.

Gone are the days when coin collecting was only a passive hobby mostly for wealthy history buffs and art lovers. The market has grown, and investors (as well as collectors) speculate on the future demand for rare coins—even making them part of their long-range investment portfolios. In fact, some people describe the rare-coin market as an "industry," no longer mainly a hobby. Either way, it's still possible to have fun and profit at the same time.

BUYER BEWARE!

Some television promotions, investment pitches, and offers to sell coins to the general public (rather than to active collectors) are priced higher than what a knowledgeable collector would pay. On top of that, remember that popular coin magazines and newspapers give no guarantee that items advertised in certain grades will merit those grades if submitted to a professional grading firm. Beware of "bargains." A bargain-priced offering might actually be a loss leader, designed to gather collector names for future offerings (bombarding you with emails, phone calls, and junk mail later). On the Internet, be aware that auction sites are a "venue" only—they don't examine coins offered for sale, and they don't guarantee they're properly graded, or even genuine.

Your best bet is to always buy from an established professional dealer or firm—as you would if you were buying a valuable painting or antique.

SOME ADVICE FROM THE EXPERTS

The editors of the best-selling *Guide Book of United States Coins*, popularly known as the "Red Book," offer this advice to collectors and investors:

Buyers must beware of overpriced or overgraded coins that simply are not worth what is charged for them. This is especially true of coins that are offered for sale online or at electronic auctions, where it often is not possible to examine the items carefully enough to determine authenticity or grade. Extreme caution is advised for anyone considering an investment in expensive coins. Investigate the person or firm with whom you are dealing. Seek professional, unbiased help with grading determinations. Satisfy yourself that the coins you select are authentic and are not priced considerably higher than is being charged by other dealers. This takes time. Do not be in a hurry. Most coins that are available today will also be available next month. Take time to track the price history and trends of coins you are most interested in purchasing.

PROTECT YOUR VALUABLE COINS

An important part of being a good investor is protecting your rare coins from deterioration and theft. The best protection for keeping coins pristine is to store

them in inert, air-tight plastic holders (the encapsulation slabs of third-party grading services are a good example), and away from paper products, cigarette smoke, wood, natural rubber, paint, and textiles such as wool and felt. Humidity greater than 75% can also be harmful and should be avoided.

When you buy coins, take physical possession of them. Insure them (homeowner's insurance often does *not* cover collectibles such as rare coins) and keep them in a secure place such as a bank safe-deposit box. There have been many frauds in which sellers of gold, rare coins, and the like have offered to hold them for the buyer and later it was found that the coins did not exist or were other than described.

KEEP GOOD RECORDS

Keep invoices and maintain a listing of your purchases for identification and tax purposes. These records are very important. You can easily capture

As you become more active in the hobby, you'll want to visit coin conventions like the Whitman Coin and Collectibles Expo held several times per year in Baltimore and Philadelphia. Reading, talking to other hobbyists, and observing the market will make you a better collector and investor.

your coins digitally with an inexpensive camera or scanner; this provides proof of identification in case of loss or theft. Note that bank storage boxes are not automatically insured. Insurance costs very little and is highly recommended.

PROFITING BEYOND DOLLARS AND CENTS

Beyond the financial aspect, as a collector or investor you can profit by investigating the background and history of the coins you buy. Coins are a mirror of history and art; they tell the story of mankind over the past 2,600 years and reflect the economic struggles, wars, prosperity, and creativity of every major nation on earth. Most traditional numismatists acquire coins for their historical, artistic, cultural, and similar appeals—as tangible links with early America, ancient Rome and Greece, the British Empire, and other connections. Today, you can easily explore the motifs, issuance, and other aspects of a coin on the Internet. It's interesting to study the lives of presidents, monarchs, and other figures depicted on coins. Often, a single coin can lead to a pleasant hour or two of research. Building a working library is also strongly recommended. Most popular coinage series such as Morgan and Peace silver dollars, various denominations of gold coins, and commemoratives, can be studied and enjoyed by reading books, with the Whitman Publishing list of numismatic titles being a fine place to start.

Purchased with care and over a period of time, nearly all specialized collections have proved to be good financial investments as well—an instance of having your cake and eating it too. More than just a few enthusiasts have called coin collecting the world's greatest hobby.

We are but the custodians of these historical relics; we must appreciate and care for them while they are in our possession. Those who treat rare coins with the consideration and respect they deserve will profit in many ways, not the least of which can be in the form of a sound financial return on their investments of time and money. Enjoy the experience!

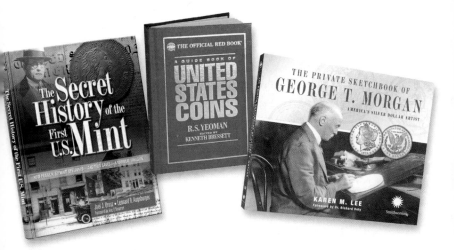

3
HOW TO GRADE YOUR COINS

A coin's "grade" is a classification of its physical condition—how much wear it's received. Such wear can come from being transported in bags from the coinage press to a storage vault, and from being circulated from hand to hand in everyday business transactions.

The *Official American Numismatic Association Grading Standards for United States Coins* describes the process of wear:

> When a coin first begins to show signs of handling, abrasion, or light wear, only the highest parts of the design are affected. Evidence that such a coin is not Uncirculated can be seen by carefully examining the high spots for signs of a slight change in color, surface texture, or sharpness of fine details.
>
> In early stages of wear the highest points of design become slightly rounded or flattened, and the very fine details begin to merge together in small spots.
>
> After a coin has been in circulation for a short time, the entire design and surface will show light wear. Many of the high parts will lose their sharpness, and most of the original mint luster will begin to wear away except in recessed areas.
>
> Further circulation will reduce the sharpness and relief of the entire design. High points then begin to merge with the next lower parts of the design.
>
> After the protective rim is worn away the entire surface becomes flat, and most of the details blend together or become partially merged with the surface.

In *Grading Coins by Photographs: An Action Guide for the Collector and Investor*, Q. David Bowers notes that "grading is perhaps the single most important factor affecting the price of a coin. Rarity is important, of course, and so is demand. However, for a given variety of large copper cent, or gold $20 double eagle, or Shield nickel, its value is affected dramatically by the grade it seems to be in. The word *seems* is appropriate, for grading is, always has been, and will forever admit of a generous proportion of, old-fashioned *opinion*. What is Gem Uncirculated or Mint State-65 to one expert can legitimately be viewed as a lower grade, MS-64, by another expert, and MS-66 by yet another. This is because grading is interpretive, not an exact science."

Simply put, knowledgeable collectors will pay more for a higher-grade, visually attractive coin than for a lower-grade, less attractive example of the same coin. The 1901 Morgan silver dollar offers a dramatic example of how grade can affect value. The following prices are from recent editions of the *Guide Book of United States Coins*:

1901 Morgan silver dollar—VF-20: $50 • EF-40: $115 • AU-50: $350 • MS-60: $2,300 • MS-63: $15,750 • MS-64: $45,000 • MS-65: $375,000

Coin grades are standardized to a 70-point scale, as endorsed by the American Numismatic Association. (For more on how this scale was developed, see *Grading Coins by Photographs* or *The Official American Numismatic Association Grading Standards for United States Coins*.)

These three 1901 Morgan silver dollars were sold at auction within a year of each other. The one at top left sold for $100; the one at top right sold for $1,000; and the one at bottom sold for more than $43,000. Their values varied because of their grades (EF-45, AU-58, and MS-64).

To grade any given coin:

1. determine its denomination (e.g., cent, dime, dollar)
2. determine what *type* it is (e.g., Indian Head cent, Barber quarter dollar)
3. find that coin type's grading standards in this book or in a grading-standards book
4. compare your coin with the text descriptions and photographs, and find the best match

Grades are assigned using an alphanumeric code—a combination of letters and numbers (for example, VG-8 or EF-40). The letters are abbreviations for these descriptions:

Abbrev.	Grade Description	Grade Number(s)	Notes
MS	Mint State	60–70	Mint State coins are collected in the full range from MS-70 (the highest quality within the grade), MS-69, MS-68, down to MS-60 (the lowest Mint State). Mint State is also known as *Uncirculated.*
AU	About Uncirculated	50–59	About Uncirculated grades usually are assigned as AU-58, AU-55, AU-53, and AU-50 (from highest quality within the grade to lowest).
EF	Extremely Fine	40–49	Typical Extremely Fine grades are EF-45 and EF-40.
VF	Very Fine	20–39	Typical Very Fine grades are VF-30 and VF-20.
F	Fine	12–19	Typical Fine grades are F-15 and F-12.
VG	Very Good	8–11	Typical Very Good grades are VG-10 and VG-8.
G	Good	4–7	Typical Good grades are G-6 and G-4.
AG	About Good	3	

Below AG-3, the lowest coin grades are Fair-2 and Poor-1.

OFFICIAL ANA GRADING TERMINOLOGY: MINT STATE COINS

To grade a Mint State coin—to accurately and consistently apply the 11-point system from MS-60 to MS-70—you need to be familiar with the specific grading standards for its particular type, its date, and the mint it was struck at. However, the broad guidelines below will give you an idea of how to grade Mint State coins in general. Beneath each grade designation is a commentary concerning certain aspects of that grade, namely *Contact Marks, Hairlines, Luster,* and *Eye Appeal.*

Contact Marks are tiny nicks, dings, and other intrusions into the metal surface of a coin. They're created when a coin comes into contact with other coins (such as in a cloth bag), in pocket change, while being stored or moved, or, in some instances, through careless handling by collectors. A coin with few or no contact marks is a candidate for a high grade, while a coin with extensive contact marks must be placed in a lower category.

Hairlines are tiny lines in the surface of a coin, sometimes visible on the higher parts such as the cheek of Miss Liberty on older coins, or in open areas of the field. They are caused by friction, cleaning, or other sliding or moving contact of a cloth or other item with a coin's surface.

Luster is one of the most important aspects of grading in the Mint State category. All other things being equal, a coin with rich, deep mint luster is a better candidate for a higher grade than is one with a dull or lifeless luster. One rule does not fit all coin types; luster can vary from type to type. To gain expertise in this vital feature, you should examine a wide selection of coins in the marketplace.

Eye Appeal is difficult to define, but most collectors know a pleasing or beautiful coin when they see one. A coin that beckons with its beauty is a candidate for a higher grade than is one that is unattractive (stained, dull, over-cleaned, or lifeless).

MS-70 • The perfect coin. Has very attractive sharp strike and original luster of the highest quality for the date and mint. No contact marks are visible under magnification. No noticeable hairlines, scuff marks, or defects. Eye appeal is attractive and outstanding. If copper, the coin is bright, with full original color.

> *Contact Marks*: None show under magnification. • *Hairlines:* None show under magnification. • *Luster:* Very attractive. Fully original. • *Eye Appeal:* Outstanding.

MS-69 • Has very attractive sharp strike and full original luster for the date and mint, with no more than two small non-detracting contact marks or flaws. No hairlines or scuff marks can be seen. Has exceptional eye appeal. If copper, the coin is bright, with original color and luster.

> *Contact Marks*: 1 or 2 minuscule. None in prime focal areas. • *Hairlines:* None visible. • *Luster:* Very attractive. Fully original. • *Eye Appeal:* Exceptional.

MS-68 • Has attractive sharp strike and full original luster for the date and mint, with no more than four light scattered contact marks or flaws. No hairlines or scuff marks show. Has exceptional eye appeal. If copper, the coin is lustrous and has original color.

> *Contact Marks*: 3 or 4 minuscule. None in prime focal areas. • *Hairlines:* None visible. • *Luster:* Attractive. Fully original. • *Eye Appeal:* Exceptional.

MS-67 • Has original luster and normal strike for date and mint. May have three or four very small contact marks and one more noticeable but not detracting mark. On comparable coins, one or two small single hairlines may show, or one or two minor scuff marks or flaws may be present. Eye appeal is above average. If copper, the coin has luster and original color.

> *Contact Marks*: 3 or 4 minuscule. 1 or 2 may be in prime focal areas. • *Hairlines:* None visible without magnification. • *Luster:* Above average. Nearly full original. • *Eye Appeal:* Exceptional.

MS-66 • Has above average quality of surface and mint luster, with no more than three or four minor or noticeable contact marks. A few light hairlines may show under magnification, or there may be one or two light scuff marks showing. Eye appeal is above average and very pleasing for the date and mint. If copper, the coin displays original or lightly toned color (which must be designated).

Contact Marks: Several small; a few may be in prime focal areas. • *Hairlines:* None visible without magnification. • *Luster:* Above average. Fully original. • *Eye Appeal:* Above average.

MS-65 • Shows an attractive high quality of luster and strike for the date and mint. May have a few small scattered contact marks, or two larger marks may be present. One or two small patches of hairlines may show. Noticeable light scuff marks may be seen on the high points of the design. Overall quality is above average and eye appeal is very pleasing. If copper, the coin has some attractive luster with original or darkened color, as designated.

Contact Marks: Light and scattered without major distracting marks in prime focal areas. • *Hairlines:* May have a few scattered. • *Luster:* Above average. Fully original. • *Eye Appeal:* Very pleasing.

MS-64 • Has at least average luster and strike for the type. Several small contact marks in groups, as well as one or two moderately heavy marks may be present. One or two small patches of hairlines may show. Noticeable light scuff marks or defects might be seen within the design or in the field. Overall quality is attractive, with a pleasing eye appeal. If copper, the coin may be slightly dull.

Contact Marks: May have light scattered marks; a few may be in prime focal areas • *Hairlines:* May have a few scattered or a small patch. • *Luster:* Average. • *Eye Appeal:* Quite attractive.

MS-63 • Mint luster may be slightly impaired. Numerous small contact marks and a few scattered heavy marks may be seen. Small hairlines are visible without magnification. Several detracting scuff marks or defects may be present throughout the design or in the fields. The general quality is about average, but overall the coin is rather attractive. Copper pieces may be darkened or dull. Color should be designated.

Contact Marks: May have distracting marks in prime focal areas. • *Hairlines:* May have a few scattered or a small patch. • *Luster:* May slightly impaired. • *Eye Appeal:* Rather attractive.

MS-62 • An impaired or dull luster may be evident. Clusters of small marks may be present throughout with a few large marks or nicks in prime focal areas. Hairlines may be very noticeable. Large unattractive scuff marks might be seen on major features. The strike, rim, and planchet quality may be noticeably below average. Overall eye appeal is below average. If copper, the coin will show a diminished color and tone.

Contact Marks: May have distracting marks in prime focal areas and/or secondary areas. • *Hairlines:* May have a few scattered or a noticeable patch. • *Luster:* May be somewhat impaired. • *Eye Appeal:* Generally acceptable.

MS-61 • Mint luster may be diminished or noticeably impaired, and the surface may have clusters of large and small contact marks throughout. Hairlines could be very noticeable. Scuff marks may show as unattractive patches on large areas or major features. Small rim nicks and striking or planchet defects may show, and the quality may be noticeably poor. Eye appeal is somewhat unattractive. Copper pieces will be generally dull, dark, and possibly spotted.

> *Contact Marks*: May have a few heavy (or numerous light) marks in prime focal and/or secondary areas. • *Hairlines:* May have noticeable patch or continuous hairlining over surfaces. • *Luster:* May be impaired. • *Eye Appeal:* Unattractive.

MS-60 • Unattractive, dull, or washed-out mint luster may mark this coin. There may be many large detracting contact marks, or damage spots, but no trace of circulation wear. There could be a heavy concentration of hairlines, or unattractive large areas of scuff marks. Rim nicks may be present, and eye appeal is very poor. Copper coins may be dark, dull, and spotted.

> *Contact Marks*: May have heavy marks in all areas. • *Hairlines:* May have noticeable patch or continuous hairlining overall. • *Luster:* Often impaired. • *Eye Appeal:* Poor.

OFFICIAL ANA GRADING TERMINOLOGY: CIRCULATED COINS

AU-58 • *Also:* Very Choice About Uncirculated-58 • The barest trace of wear may be seen on one or more of the high points of the design. No major detracting contact marks will be present and the coin will have attractive eye appeal and nearly full luster, often with the appearance of a higher grade.

AU-55 • *Also:* Choice About Uncirculated-55 • Only small patches of wear are visible on the highest points of the design. As is the case with the other grades described here, specific information is listed in the following text under the various types, for wear often occurs in different spots on different designs. Eye appeal and surface are above average.

AU-53 • *Also:* About Uncirculated-53 • Noticeable spots of wear on several high points. Very few contact marks or blemishes, and generally good eye appeal. Luster is diminished.

AU-50 • *Also:* About Uncirculated-50 • Shows traces of wear on many of the highest parts of the design. On many of these coins, some of the original mint luster is still present. May have a few noticeable contact marks or flaws.

EF-45 • *Also:* Choice Extremely Fine-45 • Has light overall wear on the coin's highest points. All design details are very sharp. Mint luster is usually seen only in protected areas of the coin's surface such as between the star point and in the letter spaces.

EF-40 • *Also:* Extremely Fine-40 • Has only slight wear but more extensive than the preceding, still with excellent overall sharpness. Traces of mint luster may still show. All design elements show clearly.

VF-35 • *Also:* Choice Very Fine-35 • Surfaces show light overall wear with minor blemishes. May have one or two small rim nicks. All details show clearly.

VF-30 • *Also:* Choice Very Fine-30 • Light even wear shows on the surface; design details on the highest points begin to soften, but all lettering and major features are bold.

VF-25 • *Also:* Very Fine-25 • Entire surface shows light signs of wear and softening of design elements. Major features are strong and clear. Some of the minor details blend into the design.

VF-20 • *Also:* Very Fine-20 • Moderate noticeable wear on the higher parts of the design. Minor details are beginning to flatten. Surfaces are attractive and free of serious blemishes, erosion, nicks, or scratches.

F-15 • *Also:* Fine-15 • Shows moderate even wear through the surface. Entire design is bold and clear with traces of flattening.

F-12 • *Also:* Fine-12 • Moderate to considerable even wear. Entire design is bold. All lettering, including the word LIBERTY (on coins with this feature on the shield or headband), is visible, but may show only parts of the letters.

VG-10 • *Also:* Very Good-10 • Even wear throughout the entire coin. Parts of the rim may be flat but still discernable. Some of the letters in LIBERTY are readable.

VG-8 • *Also:* Very Good-8 • Well worn. Major design elements are visible, but with faintness in areas. Head of Liberty, wreath, and other major features are visible in outline form without center detail. LIBERTY is mostly worn away.

G-6 • *Also:* Good-6 • Heavily worn, but with clean attractive surfaces and no major blemishes. May have a few rim nicks and scratches. Rim is very weak but basically complete.

G-4 • *Also:* Good-4 • Heavily worn. Major design elements are visible, but with faintness in areas. Head of Liberty, wreath, and other major features, as applicable, are visible in outline form, without center detail. Rims may be incomplete in spots.

AG-3 • *Also:* About Good-3 • Very heavily worn, with portions of the lettering, date, and legends worn smooth. The date is barely readable. Rims merge into the lettering.

Fair-2 • Most of the design details are worn completely smooth. Much of the legend and date are merged into the field. Rims are flat or missing. May have serious nicks, dents, and defects.

Poor-1 • Only the basic coin type is identifiable. Date and mintmark must be strong enough to be readable. Entire surface is worn and may be disfigured by numerous blemishes.

4
PROOF COINS

The term *Proof* (capitalized) refers to a manufacturing process and not a grade. Proof coins are struck at the U.S. Mint by a special process from carefully prepared dies, sharp in all features. The flat surfaces of the dies are given a high mirror-like polish. Specially prepared planchets (round blanks of metal for coinage) are fed into low-speed coining presses. Each Proof coin is slowly and carefully struck more than once, to accentuate its details. When striking is completed the coin is taken from the press with care and not allowed to come into contact with other pieces. The result is a coin with mirror-like surfaces.

From 1817 through 1857, Proof coins were made only on special occasions and were not for general sale to collectors. They were made available to visiting foreign dignitaries, government officials, and those with connections at the Mint. (Earlier, pre-1817, U.S. coins may have prooflike surfaces and many Proof characteristics, but they were not specifically or intentionally struck as Proofs. These are sometimes designated as *specimen strikes.*) Beginning in 1858, Proofs were sold to collectors openly. In that year 80 silver Proof sets (containing silver coins from the three-cent piece through the silver dollar), plus additional pieces of the silver dollar denomination, were produced, as well as perhaps 200 (the exact number is not known) copper-nickel cents and a limited number of Proof gold coins.

The traditional mirror-like or "brilliant" type of Proof finish was used on all U.S. Proof coins of the 1800s. During the 1900s, cents through the 1909 Indian Head, nickels through the 1912 Liberty Head, regular-issue silver coins through 1915, and gold coins through 1907 were of the brilliant mirror-like format. When modern Proof coinage was resumed in 1936 and continued through 1942, then 1950 to 1964, and 1968 to date, the brilliant mirror-like finish was used. While these types of Proofs are referred to as "brilliant Proofs," actual specimens may have toned over the years. The mirror-like surface is still evident, however.

From 1908 through 1915, Matte Proofs and Sand Blast Proofs (the latter created by directing fine sand particles at high pressure toward the coin's surface) were made of certain gold coins (exceptions are 1909 and 1910 Proofs with Satin Finish). While characteristics vary from issue to issue, generally all of these pieces have extreme sharpness of design detail and sharp, squared-off rims. The surfaces are without luster and have a dullish matte

A Proof 1951 Franklin half dollar. Note the brilliant mirror-like surfaces.

surface. Sand Blast Proofs were made of certain commemorative coins also, such as the 1928 Hawaiian half dollar.

Satin Finish (sometimes called *Roman Finish*) Proof gold coins were made in 1909 and 1910. These pieces are sharply struck, have squared-off edges, and have a satin-like surface finish, not too much different from an Uncirculated coin (which causes confusion among collectors today, and

A Proof 1937 Wheat cent.

which at the time of issue was quite unpopular as collectors resented having to pay a premium for a coin without a distinctly different appearance).

Matte Proofs were made of Lincoln cents of 1909 to 1916 and Buffalo nickels of 1913 to 1916. Such coins have extremely sharp design detail, squared-off rims, "brilliant" (mirrorlike) edges, but a matte or satin-like (or even full satin, not with flashy mint luster) surface. In some instances Matte Proof dies may have been used to make regular circulation strikes after the requisite number of Matte Proofs was made for collectors. So, it is important that a Matte Proof, to be considered authentic, have squared-off rims and mirror-like perfect edges in addition to the proper surface characteristics.

GRADING PROOF COINS

The mirror-like surfaces of a brilliant Proof coin are much more susceptible to damage than are the surfaces of an Uncirculated coin. Proofs are divided into classifications from Proof-60 (a Proof with handling marks, but without wear) continuously through Proof-70 (a coin with no hairlines, handling marks, or other defects; in other words, a flawless coin. Such a coin may be brilliant or may have natural toning).

As the mirror fields used for most Proofs tend to be very susceptible to mishandling and to show marks, whereas the frosty luster of a Mint State coin can often conceal marks, eye appeal diminishes rapidly as Proof grades go below Proof-65.

PF-65 • *Also:* Gem Proof • Surfaces are brilliant, with no noticeable blemishes or flaws. A few scattered, but barely noticeable, marks or hairlines.

PF-63 • *Also:* Choice Proof • Surfaces are reflective, with only a few blemishes in secondary focal places. No major flaws.

PF-60 • Surfaces may have several contact marks, hairlines, or light rubs. Luster may be dull and eye appeal lacking.

5

THIRD-PARTY GRADING AND AUTHENTICATION

In this book, values from under $1 up to several hundred dollars are for "raw" coins—that is, coins that have *not* been graded and encapsulated by a professional third-party grading service. Coins valued near or above $500 are assumed to be third-party-graded. A high-value coin that has not been professionally certified as authentic, graded, and encapsulated by an independent firm is apt to be valued lower than the prices indicated.

What *is* third-party grading? This is a service providing, for a fee, an impartial, independent opinion of a coin's grade and its authenticity. The grader is neither buyer nor seller (hence "third-party"), and has no biased interest in the

Many high-grade and valuable coins in today's marketplace are "slabbed"—carefully graded, authenticated, and encapsulated in plastic by professional grading firms.

coin's market value. Third-party grading started in the late 1970s with ANACS (then a service of the American Numismatic Association; now privately owned and operated). ANACS graders would examine a coin and, after determining its authenticity, would assign separate grades to its obverse and reverse (such as MS-63/65) and return it to the sender, along with a certificate and photograph.

In 1986 a group of coin dealers launched the Professional Coin Grading Service (PCGS), which grades coins for a fee and hermetically seals them in plastic holders with interior labels. This "slabbing" helps guarantee that a coin and its grade certificate cannot be separated. In 1987 Numismatic Guaranty Corporation of America (NGC) was started, offering a similar encapsulation service. Both companies unconditionally guarantee the authenticity and grades of the coins they certify. Coins are judged by consensus, with the graders having no knowledge of who submitted them.

From the 1970s to the present there have been more than 100 different commercial grading companies. Readers are cautioned to investigate the background of a TPG (third-party grader) before trusting in its services. Today the hobby's leading third-party grading firms are NGC (Sarasota, Florida) and PCGS (Newport Beach, California).

Professional grading strives to be completely objective, but coins are graded by humans and not computers. This introduces a subjective element of *art* as opposed to pure *science* or technicality. A coin's grade, even if certified by a leading TPG, can be questioned by any collector or dealer—or even by the service that graded it, if resubmitted for a second look. Furthermore, within a given grade, a keen observer will find coins that are low-quality, average, and high-quality for that grade. Such factors as luster, color, strength of strike, and overall eye appeal can make, for example, one MS-65 1891 Morgan dollar more visually attractive than another with the same grade. This gives the smart collector the opportunity to "cherrypick," or examine multiple slabbed coins and select the highest-quality coin for the desired grade. This process builds a better collection than simply accepting a TPG's assigned grades, and is summed up in the guidance of "Buy the coin, not the slab." (Also note that a coin certified as, for example, MS-64 might have greater eye appeal—and therefore be more desirable to a greater number of collectors—than a less attractive coin graded MS-65 or even higher.)

Over the years, collectors have observed a trend nicknamed "gradeflation": the more liberal reinterpretation, in practice, of the standards applied to a given grade over time. For example, a coin evaluated by a leading TPG in 1992 as MS-64 might be graded today as MS-65 or even MS-66.

The general effect of third-party grading and authentication has been to increase buyers' and sellers' comfort levels with the perceived quality of rare coins in the marketplace. And, as mentioned, there still exists the potential for keen-eyed collectors to seek out the best and cherrypick slabbed coins that are "exceptional for their grade."

6
COLLECTING COLONIAL AND EARLY AMERICAN COINS

As we saw in chapter 1, money had a rich history in America even before the United States struck its first national coinage in 1792. When coins came off the presses from the first Philadelphia Mint, Americans were much more accustomed to legal tender from other countries. People accepted coins, both old and new, whose value was based more on the metal content than on the issuer's reliability. Foreign money in America during the colonial period had become so embedded that it continued to be accepted as legal tender until discontinued by law in 1857. Coins of this era are so fundamental to American numismatics that every collection should include at least a sampling.

Many of the foreign coins from England, Spain, Portugal, France, Germany, and the Netherlands have names, sizes, and expressions whose usage has continued to the present day. Not only did the popular Spanish-American silver 8 reales become a model for the American silver dollar, but its fractional parts morphed into the half-dollar and quarter-dollar coins that are now common fractions of the U.S. dollar. It was not until 1997 that stock-market prices ceased being quoted in the Spanish-real system of eighths of a dollar. Similarly, the American one-cent coin has never totally lost its association with the English penny, and non-collectors still call it by that name.

The use of foreign coins was so prevalent in colonial times that the dollar sign and the very term *dollar*, as we know them today, did not come into general use until 1767. The paper dollars printed by Maryland and issued that year were the first to include the term to indicate the Spanish-American piece of eight. This was a radical departure from denominations in terms of English pounds, shillings, and pence.

It was no simple task to distinguish between the relative values of the multitude of circulating foreign currencies. English, Portuguese, Spanish, German, Dutch, and other coins all had to be calculated in terms that related to their values in various colonies and states. To facilitate conversions, books and published charts showed comparison prices for each currency. In mid-1750, for instance, the Spanish dollar was quoted as being worth eight shillings in New York, but sixpence less in New Jersey, and only four shillings, eightpence in Georgia.

Many kinds of private and state issues of coins and tokens filtered into commerce during the colonial period from 1616 to 1776. They are the true essence of collectible money of that era. These are items that catch the attention and imagination of everyone interested in the history and development of early America. But even with their enormous historical importance, you can form a basic collection of these pieces of Americana; it's not nearly as daunting as you might expect.

Many collectors use the *Guide Book of United States Coins* (the hobby's annually issued "Red Book") to form a set of colonial and early American coins. The Red Book is not encyclopedic in its scope, but it includes more than 50 pages covering British New World issues, coinage authorized by British royal patent, early American and related tokens, French New World issues, coinage of the states, private tokens from after confederation, and George Washington medals and tokens. Beyond the basic types are numerous sub-varieties of some of the issues, and a wide range of European coins. Collectors attempt to accumulate as many of those as their time and finances permit. Some aim for the finest possible condition, while others find great enjoyment in pieces that saw actual circulation and were obviously used during the formative days of the country. Many can be bought for $10 to $50; rarities sell for tens or hundreds of thousands of dollars—even millions. There are no rules about how or what to collect other than to enjoy owning a genuine piece of early American history.

This sampling shows just a few of the coins and tokens of the colonies and early United States. For more information, see the *Guide Book of United States Coins* or the *Whitman Encyclopedia of Colonial and Early American Coins.*

The first colonial coins struck in New England were from Massachusetts, 1652. This is a sixpence—one of eight known to have survived over the centuries. Each is worth roughly $35,000 to more than $200,000.

In the mid- to late 1600s Massachusetts struck coins with willow trees, oak trees, and pine trees on them. This Pine Tree shilling, though dated 1652, is from the era of 1675–1682. Values range from $600 or so in Good condition up to $24,000 or more in Mint State.

The famous New England Elephant tokens are believed to have been struck in England to promote interest in the American colonies. An example in Fine condition is worth $100,000 or more.

Bar coppers—undated and of uncertain origin—date from around 1785. They feature a design nearly identical to that used on a Continental Army uniform button during the Revolutionary War.

Jola tokens were authorized by the military governor of San Antonio, Texas, in 1818. Eight thousand of them were struck, though far fewer survive today. These small coins are worth up to $18,500—perhaps more—depending on their condition.

Many patriotic tokens and medals were privately struck in the early 1780s through the mid-1790s with designs honoring General (later President) George Washington. They can be collected for prices ranging from $75 or so well into six figures.

7
HALF CENTS AND LARGE CENTS

As strange as it sounds today, for more than 60 years the U.S. Mint struck *half-cent* coins. These copper pieces have the smallest denomination of all the nation's coinage. Today at face value one wouldn't even buy a gumball, but they had purchasing power back when the average worker made about $1 a day in wages. Also, the Spanish milled dollar (see chapter 1) was equal to eight reales—each real being worth 12-1/2 cents—so the little half-cent coin was useful for making change.

Half cents were among the first coins produced by the Philadelphia Mint, starting in 1793. The Mint also struck large copper *cents* starting that year. Early on, these coins were made from hand-engraved dies, often on copper planchets of varying quality, by two men tugging on the weighted lever arm of a small screw-type coining press. Finally in 1836 steam power was introduced to run the Mint's presses. In a typical year the half cents were struck in the tens or hundreds of thousands, along with mintage of between two million and seven million large cents.

By the mid-1850s the cost of making and distributing these copper coins was too expensive for the Mint—Director James Ross Snowden reported that they "barely paid expenses." The coins had also grown unpopular, and they scarcely circulated outside of the nation's larger cities. In 1857 the Mint abandoned the large cent (replacing it with a smaller copper-nickel cent) and stopped making half cents entirely.

Today collectors enjoy these beautiful and unusual pieces of early Americana. There are several types, or major designs, of both the half cent and the large cent. Our coverage in this book is fairly high-level, because these coins are *not* commonly found in everyday coin collections. For more detailed information, including values for every date and more grades, consult the *Guide Book of United States Coins* (the "Red Book").

TYPICAL VALUES FOR HALF CENTS AND LARGE CENTS

These are prices you'll typically see for the most common dates of each major type of half cent and large cent, in various conditions.

HALF CENTS	G-4	F-12	EF-40	AU-50	MS-60	MS-63	MS-65	PF-60
Liberty Cap, 1793	$3,250	$8,500	$25,000	$38,000	$65,000	$95,000		
Liberty Cap, 1794–1797	475	1,100	4,100	7,200	16,000			
Draped Bust, 1800–1808	70	120	325	675	1,200	2,900	$7,500	
Classic Head, 1809–1836	50	70	120	175	300	750	1,250	$5,000
Braided Hair, 1840–1857	45	65	100	165	275	450	1,000	3,400

LARGE CENTS	G-4	F-12	EF-40	MS-60	MS-63	MS-65	PF-63	PF-65
Chain, 1793	$7,200	$17,500	$53,000	$195,000				
Wreath, 1793	2,500	5,000	15,000	55,000	$100,000			
Liberty Cap, 1793–1796	325	650	3,000	8,200	20,000			
Draped Bust, 1796–1807	60	165	1,000	3,000	8,500	$27,500		
Classic Head, 1808–1814	50	240	1,400	4,750	10,000			
Matron Head, 1816–1835	20	32	125	350	550	1,300	$14,500	$40,000
Matron Head Modified, 1835–1839	20	32	110	325	500	1,200	14,000	38,000
Braided Hair, 1839–1857	18	25	60	180	230	650	5,000	12,000

For general grading instructions for these neat old copper coins, see the chapter on "How to Grade Your Coins." The important areas to look at are the details in Miss Liberty's hair, and the centers and details of the leaves on the reverse. You'll find more in-depth instructions for each specific coin type in *Grading Coins by Photographs*, by Q. David Bowers. The following illustrations will give you an idea of what a Good, Very Fine, and Mint State coin looks like.

G-4 half cent, Classic Head type (shown enlarged).

VF-20 half cent, Braided Hair type (shown enlarged).

MS-63 half cent, Classic Head type (shown enlarged).

G-4 large cent, Classic Head type (shown enlarged).

VF-20 large cent, Braided Hair type (shown enlarged).

MS-63 large cent, Matron Head type (shown enlarged).

EARLY HALF CENTS
(1790s)

There are two types of half cents dating from the 1790s: the Liberty Cap, Head Facing Left (struck only in 1793), and the Liberty Cap, Head Facing Right (struck from 1794 to 1797).

Liberty Cap half cent, Head Facing Left (1793).

The first type is scarce in all grades, and difficult even for active collectors to locate—after 200-plus years, perhaps 500 to 1,000 of the 1793 coins still exist, out of 35,334 minted. Collectors will pay about $1,650 for a well-worn, AG-3 example (worn nearly smooth, but with details clear enough to identify the coin) . . . about $5,000 for a VG-8 (with some details in Miss Liberty's hair, and the reverse lettering completely visible) . . . and $38,000 for an AU-50 coin (with only a trace of wear on Liberty's face).

Liberty Cap half cent, Head Facing Right (1794–1797).

The second type also is scarce, with perhaps 4,000 to 6,000 coins still kicking around. If you find a 1794–1797 half cent in Grandpa's cigar box, or want to add one to your own collection, you can expect to see values of about $650 for a common date in VG-8, up to $23,000-plus in MS-63.

DRAPED BUST HALF CENTS
(1800–1808)

Draped Bust half cents, as a type, are more readily available to collectors (up to and including examples in Mint State) than those of the 1790s.

A more common date, such as the 1804, is worth about $75 in G-4 condition (with the outline of Miss Liberty's bust clear, the date readable, and the reverse lettering worn and incomplete) . . . about $200 in VF-20 (with only slight wear in the shoulder drapery and the hair over Liberty's brow, and slight wear on the reverse) . . . and about $1,200 in MS-60 (with brown color, slight abrasions on the higher parts of Liberty's portrait, and some red-orange mint luster in the fields).

Draped Bust half cent (1800–1808).

CLASSIC HEAD HALF CENTS
(1809–1836)

Early dates of the Classic Head half cent are often seen lightly struck (with softer details, especially in the portrait). Later dates (in the 1820s and 1830s) are usually well struck. An estimated 35,000 to 45,000 of these coins still exist in circulated grades, and another 5,000 to 8,000 in Mint State.

Classic Head half cent (1809–1836).

The most common dates (e.g., those of the 1830s) can be bought for about $50 in VG-8 (with the word LIBERTY entirely visible on the hair band, and the lower curls of hair worn) . . . about $85 in VF-20 (with the lettering clear-cut and the hair only lightly worn) . . . or about $300 in MS-60 (mostly brown in color but with reddish-orange mint luster in the fields, and no trace of wear but some slight abrasions on Liberty's face).

BRAIDED HAIR HALF CENTS
(1840–1857)

Early dates of the Classic Head half cent are often seen lightly struck (with softer details, especially in the portrait). Later dates (in the 1820s and 1830s) are usually well struck. An estimated 35,000 to 45,000 of these coins still exist in circulated grades, and another 5,000 to 8,000 in Mint State.

Braided Hair half cent (1840–1857).

The most common dates (e.g., those of the 1830s) can be bought for about $50 in VG-8 (with the word LIBERTY entirely visible on the hair band, and the lower curls of hair worn) . . . about $85 in VF-20 (with the lettering clear-cut and the hair only lightly worn) . . . or about $300 in MS-60 (mostly brown in color but with reddish-orange mint luster in the fields, and no trace of wear but some slight abrasions on Liberty's face).

EARLY LARGE CENTS
(1790S AND EARLY 1800S)

The Flowing Hair design was used on large cents of 1793, with two different reverse: the Chain Reverse and the Wreath Reverse.

Flowing Hair large cent, Chain Reverse (1793).

Wreath Reverse, Regular Sprig.

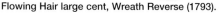

Flowing Hair large cent, Wreath Reverse (1793).

Wreath Reverse, Strawberry Leaf.

The chain design was not popular in the United States, which was still a young nation with the memory of British rule smarting. Some Americans criticized the chain as a sign of slavery or oppression, rather than a symbol of strength through unity. Only 36,103 of the coins were minted before the design was changed to the Wreath Reverse. Of those, a mere 700 to 1,000 have survived the ensuing centuries, the rest being worn too smooth to identify, melted to make new coins, or otherwise lost to history. Even AG-3 examples (well worn, but with the date and design elements clear enough to identify) will sell for $2,900 to $4,000 or so . . . while a VG-8 example will bring $13,000 to $17,000 . . . and a VF-20 coin is worth upwards of $45,000. In AU and Mint State (with perhaps two dozen estimated to still exist), the 1793 large cent easily hits six-figure values.

The Wreath Reverse large cents of 1793 are rare but popular among collectors. Typical grades are Good (hair worn smooth except the thick tresses at left; worth about $2,500) to Fine (about one-third of the hair's details visible; worth about $5,000). A super-rare variety (only four examples known!) is the "Strawberry Leaf," one of which sold for $862,500 in January 2009.

From mid-1793 partway through 1796, the Mint struck large cents of the Liberty Cap type. Those dated 1793 are rare and in great demand, while the others are more readily available. All together some 14,000 to 18,000 are estimated to exist in circulated conditions, and another 400 to 700 in Mint State.

Liberty Cap large cent (1793–1796).

The 1795 is the most commonly seen date; in AG-3 condition (the portrait visible only as an outline, LIBERTY partially worn away, and the date weak but discernible) the 1795 is worth about $100. The value increases to $425 in VG-8 (with some hair detail visible in the lower areas, and LIBERTY and the date bold) . . . around $1,350 in VF-20 (with hair details stronger but indistinct or flat at the center) . . . while a nice MS-63 example (with no abrasion visible, and the color brown with original mint luster) can bring $20,000 or more.

Most of the Draped Bust large cents, minted from 1796 to 1807, are plentiful in lower grades (commonly ranging from Good to Fine). Mint State examples are very scarce, and are generally in lower grades, MS-60 to MS-63, with brown surfaces. A more common date, such as

Draped Bust large cent (1796–1807).

the 1803, is worth about $35 in AG-3 condition (smooth, but with details clear enough to identify) . . . about $120 in VG-8 (with the drapery on Miss Liberty partly visible) . . . and $165 in VF-20 (with the hair lines lightly worn).

Classic Head large cents often are found poorly struck, with weak details, and the later dates typically have dark and porous surfaces (from the low-quality copper used to make them after the War of 1812 started and Great Britain stopped exporting high-quality coin

Classic Head large cent (1808–1814).

planchets to the United States). Still, examples are readily available for collectors, in circulated grades up to Very Fine and Extremely Fine. The more common pieces are worth about $22 in AG-3 (worn, but with enough details to identify) . . . $85 or so in VG-8 (with LIBERTY readable, and Miss Liberty's ear visible) . . . and $250 in F-12 (with the forehead hair nearly smooth but the ear, and the hair under it, sharp). Values bump up sharply in higher grades: $600 in VF-20 (with some detail in all the hair lines, and only slight wear on the leaves on the reverse) . . . $1,400 in EF-40 (with all hair lines sharp, and very slight wear on the high points of the design) . . . and $4,750 in MS-60 (with some slight abrasions on the portrait, complex detail visible in the hair, and complete or nearly complete mint luster on the coin's surface). In January 2012 an MS-63 Classic Head large cent of 1813 sold at auction for $10,925—not bad for a $0.01 investment carefully preserved for 200 years!

LATER LARGE CENTS
(1816–1857)

The U.S. Mint took a break from large cents and didn't make any in 1815. From 1816 into the 1850s it struck the coins in various incarnations of the Liberty Head design, showing the profile portrait of a young woman wearing a head-band or coronet inscribed LIBERTY. These strikings include some Proofs, which are quite rare and not commonly collected. The large copper cent ended in 1857, being replaced that year with a smaller one-cent coin in copper-nickel (see next chapter).

Liberty Head large cents are easy to find in all grades. Hoards of some dates, particularly 1850 to 1856, were found over the years, making them more common today in Mint State than you might expect. Examples in G-4 condition (with the details on Miss Liberty's head partly visible, and even wear in the date and legends) can be purchased for $18 to $20, and prices ramp up slowly as the grade gets better. In EF-40 (with sharp details in the hair) a common date might be $60 or $65 . . . and in low-end Mint State (MS-60 to 63, with some slight abra-

Liberty Head, Matron Head, large cent (1816–1839). A modified version, slightly different from that pictured, was made 1837–1839.

Liberty Head, Braided Hair, large cent (1839–1857).

sions on Liberty's cheek or elsewhere on the portrait, and luster in the field complete or nearly so), a nice coin can be worth $180 to $300 or so.

8
SMALL CENTS

On May 25, 1857, the new small-diameter (19 mm) cent made its debut, replacing the copper large cent that had been minted since the 1790s. Collectors often focus on the first two series (the Flying Eagle and Indian Head cents) together. These were minted through 1909. A new design in 1909 honored President Abraham Lincoln (in the 100th anniversary of his birth). The long-lived Lincoln cent has gone through several design modifications and changes in composition over the decades.

The small cent is perhaps the most popular of all American coin denominations, and has been the jumping-off point for millions of coin collections. If you know what to look for (and you will, after reading this chapter!), you can pick scarce and valuable varieties out of your pocket change. Who wouldn't want to find a $100 coin for a penny?

James Barton Longacre (chief engraver of the U.S. Mint from 1844 to 1869) was the designer of the Flying Eagle cent, the smaller coin that replaced the copper large cent in 1857. Longacre also designed the Indian Head cent— as well as the two-cent piece, silver and nickel three-cent pieces, the Shield nickel, several pattern coins, and various gold coins. This watercolor portrait, circa the 1840s, is by the artist himself.

This chapter will introduce you to the world of small cents. You'll read more detailed information, including values for every date and more grades, in the *Guide Book of United States Coins* (the "Red Book").

These are prices you'll typically see for the most common dates of each major type of small cent, in various conditions.

SMALL CENTS	G-4	F-12	EF-40	MS-60	MS-63	MS-65	PF-63	PF-65
Flying Eagle, 1856–1858	$28.00	$45.00	$150.00	$380.00	$900.00	$4,200	$8,000	$25,000
Indian Head, copper-nickel, 1859	15.00	25.00	110.00	250.00	550.00	3,500	1,600	4,900
Indian Head, copper-nickel, 1860–1864	12.00	20.00	45.00	100.00	160.00	1,000	900	2,500
Indian Head, 1864–1909	1.50	4.50	10.00	38.00	55.00	170	200	1,200
Lincoln, Wheat, 1909–1958	.03	.04	.05	.10	.30	1	10	15

FLYING EAGLE CENTS

(1856–1858)

The Flying Eagle cent was designed by the Mint's chief engraver, James B. Longacre, who was inspired by an earlier eagle used on the silver dollar of 1836. The cent's reverse shows an agricultural wreath of various American products—tobacco, wheat, corn, and cotton.

Flying Eagle cent (1856–1858).

Not only were these new coins smaller than the earlier large cents, they were also of a different composition: 88 percent copper and 12 percent nickel, instead of pure copper.

Flying Eagle cents dated 1856 are actually pattern coins—struck by the Mint to show Congressmen how the new coin would look. Additional Proofs were also struck for sale to collectors. An estimated 2,000 to 3,000 of the 1856 coins were made in all. These patterns are popular among collectors who can afford them, and have traditionally been collected along with the regular issues of 1857 and 1858.

The following illustrations show what a Good, Very Fine, and Mint State Flying Eagle cent looks like.

━━ GRADING FLYING EAGLE CENTS ━━

G-4 (Good)—All details worn, but readable.

VG-8 (Very Good)—Details in eagle's feathers and eye evident, but worn.

F-12 (Fine)—Eagle-head details and feather tips sharp.

VF-20 (Very Fine)—Considerable detail visible in feathers in right wing and tail.

EF-40 (Extremely Fine)—Slight wear; all details sharp.

AU-50 (About Uncirculated)—Slight wear on eagle's left wing and breast.

MS-60 (Uncirculated)—No trace of wear. Light blemishes.

MS-63 (Choice Uncirculated)—Some distracting marks or blemishes in prime focal areas. Some impairment of luster possible.

PF-63 (Choice Proof)—Nearly perfect.

G-6 Flying Eagle cent (shown enlarged).

VF-20 Flying Eagle cent (shown enlarged).

MS-65 Flying Eagle cent (shown enlarged).

As a type the Flying Eagle cent is easy to find, mostly in worn grades. An average G-4 example is worth about $28 or $30 . . . a VF-20 about $60 . . . and an MS-60 about $380. Many varieties are known for 1857 and 1858. In particular, 1858 is found with two major variations: Large Letters (with the A and M in AMERICA joined) and Small Letters (with the letters separated). Minor variations of the wreath on the reverse also exist.

In a variety known as the 1858, 8 Over 7, you can see a small dot above the first 8 in 1858 and the ghost of a numeral 7 above the second 8 (caused when an old coinage die was ground down during production until the 7 was nearly invisible). This particular variety is worth about $75 in G-4 . . . $400 in VF-20 . . . and $3,400 in MS-60.

INDIAN HEAD CENTS
(1859–1909)

The Indian Head design for the cent, first issued in 1859, is actually a representation of Miss Liberty wearing an Indian headdress—not a true Native American. The first year featured a laurel wreath on the reverse. This was later changed to an oak wreath with a small shield at top.

Indian Head cent, copper-nickel,
Laurel Wreath Reverse,
Without Shield (1859 only).

During the American Civil War (1861–1865), nearly all gold and silver coins, and eventually even copper-nickel cents, were pulled from circulation and hoarded in the Midwest and East by people worried about the Union's future. In larger cities, various merchants stepped in to fill the need for small change by privately issuing thin, copper, cent-sized tokens. The federal government outlawed these tokens with the Act of April 22, 1864, and, recognizing their popularity, introduced its own thin, bronze one-cent coin. It continued the same design as the copper-nickel Indian Head cent, and was minted well into the first decade of the new century.

Indian Head cent, copper-nickel,
Oak Wreath Reverse,
With Shield (1860–1864).

The following illustrations show what an Indian Head cent looks like in Good, Very Fine, and Mint State condition.

Indian Head cent, bronze,
Oak Wreath Reverse,
With Shield (1864–1909).

▬ GRADING INDIAN HEAD CENTS ▬

G-4 (Good)—LIBERTY is not visible on the headdress.

VG-8 (Very Good)—At least some letters of LIBERTY are readable.

F-12 (Fine)—LIBERTY is mostly visible.

VF-20 (Very Fine)—LIBERTY has slight but even wear.

EF-40 (Extremely Fine)—LIBERTY is sharp. All other details are sharp. The end of the ribbon has only slight wear.

AU-50 (About Uncirculated)—There is a very slight trace of wear above the ear and the lowest curl of hair.

MS-60 (Uncirculated)—No trace of wear. Light blemishes.

MS-63 (Choice Uncirculated)—Some distracting marks or blemishes in prime focal areas. Some impairment of luster possible.

PF-63 (Choice Proof)—Nearly perfect.

G-4 Indian Head cent (shown enlarged).

VF-30 Indian Head cent (shown enlarged).

MS-66 Indian Head cent (shown enlarged).

The Indian Head cent was a workhorse of American commerce and could still be collected from pocket change as late as into the 1930s. As a result, these coins are often seen in worn grades. A common G-4 example is worth $1 to $2 or so . . . in VF-20, about $6 . . . and in MS-60, $38 or $40. In many years, especially from the late 1870s on, tens of millions of cents were made annually (topping out at more than 108 million struck in 1907), so even Mint State examples are plentiful.

Many die varieties exist and are very popular to collect. (See the *Cherrypickers' Guide to Rare Die Varieties.*) Some varieties to look for include an 1873 with the word LIBERTY doubled (worth more than $200 in Good condition); an 1888 with the final 8 struck over a 7 (worth $1,000 or more in Good); and an 1894 with the date doubled ($30 in Good).

An interesting story is attached to one particular variety. In 1875, Mint officials suspected a longtime employee was stealing Indian Head cents. They secretly modified a reverse die by making a small gouge in the N in ONE, and then put the die into production one morning. Later that day the suspect employee was called aside and asked to empty his pockets. Inside were 33 of the marked cents. At first he insisted his son gave him the coins, but when confronted with the secretly marked die, he admitted his guilt. He resigned in disgrace after more than 50 years of service to the Mint. Today specialists hunt for the 1875 "Dot Reverse" Indian Head cent connected to this story. In April 2012 an example was auctioned for $700 in AU-50 condition. (A regular 1875 Indian Head cent might be worth $160 in that grade.) This goes to show you: it can pay to carefully examine your coins!

LINCOLN CENTS, WHEAT EARS REVERSE
(1909–1958)

A new one-cent coin debuted in 1909, commemorating the 100th anniversary of the birth of Abraham Lincoln. Over the years this popular, affordable coin has launched more collections than probably any other type. Starting in the

Lincoln cent, Variety 1,
bronze (1909–1942).

Lincoln cent, Variety 2,
steel (1943).

Lincoln cent, Variety 1 resumed,
bronze (1944–1958).

1930s, Whitman Publishing and other companies made "penny boards" for collectors to assemble a set of Lincoln cents, by date and mintmark, from their pocket change. This was a fun and inexpensive pastime during the Great Depression. Later, Whitman innovated with multiple-panel folders and albums to store and display collections of Lincoln cents (as well as other coins). Today it's common to find old blue folders filled (or partially filled) with "Wheat" cents that someone, years ago, picked out of circulation. The coins are plentiful, and can still be purchased in quantity from dealers, by the 50-coin roll or even in 5,000-coin bags. These bulk lots typically contain Wheat cents from the 1950s, when hundreds of millions (or even billions) of coins were struck each year.

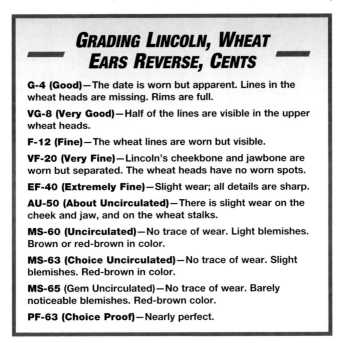

GRADING LINCOLN, WHEAT EARS REVERSE, CENTS

G-4 (Good)—The date is worn but apparent. Lines in the wheat heads are missing. Rims are full.

VG-8 (Very Good)—Half of the lines are visible in the upper wheat heads.

F-12 (Fine)—The wheat lines are worn but visible.

VF-20 (Very Fine)—Lincoln's cheekbone and jawbone are worn but separated. The wheat heads have no worn spots.

EF-40 (Extremely Fine)—Slight wear; all details are sharp.

AU-50 (About Uncirculated)—There is slight wear on the cheek and jaw, and on the wheat stalks.

MS-60 (Uncirculated)—No trace of wear. Light blemishes. Brown or red-brown in color.

MS-63 (Choice Uncirculated)—No trace of wear. Slight blemishes. Red-brown in color.

MS-65 (Gem Uncirculated)—No trace of wear. Barely noticeable blemishes. Red-brown color.

PF-63 (Choice Proof)—Nearly perfect.

The following illustrations show what a Lincoln, Wheat Ears Reverse, cent looks like in Good, Very Fine, and Mint State condition.

G-4 Lincoln, Wheat Ears Reverse, cent (shown enlarged).

VF-20 Lincoln, Wheat Ears Reverse, cent (shown enlarged).

Mint State Lincoln, Wheat Ears Reverse, cent (shown enlarged).

Wheat cents of 1909 are easily found in Mint State, because many people saved the coins as souvenirs from the first year of issue. Later dates are scarcer in high grades, although Philadelphia examples were made in higher quantities and are seen more often. Beginning in the 1930s, collectors saved bank-wrapped rolls of Mint State cents in large quantities (starting mainly in 1934, though the low-mintage 1931-S was also hoarded). Dates of the later 1930s, the 1940s, and the 1950s are all plentiful—though some are more so than others, and there are a number of scarce and rare varieties.

Collector demand is intense for scarcer Wheat cents and higher-grade examples, resulting in a strong market.

As mentioned, common-date Wheat cents can be bought in large quantities. In bulk the coins can retail for $0.03 to $0.05 apiece (between $150 and $250 for a 5,000-coin bag, although shipping costs can be an additional factor), with typical grades being VG or Fine up to lower-end Mint State. Most rolls and bags of the coins have been searched by dealers or collectors over the years, with older and scarcer dates and varieties picked out—although sometimes treasures still can be found. Here are some coins to look for:

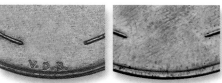

Designer's initials, V.D.B. (1909 reverse only).

No V.D.B. on reverse (1909–1958).

Mintmark location.

Designer's initials placed on Lincoln's shoulder, next to rim, starting in 1918.

1909, V.D.B.—The very first Lincoln cents included the initials of the designer, Victor David Brenner, on the reverse. When the secretary of the Treasury noticed this, he demanded that the initials be removed. There was a "feverish scramble," as the *New York Times* put it, for the new coins—Americans everywhere thought the cents would be discontinued and become an overnight rarity! The U.S. Mint made enough to meet the demand, though, and today this first-year issue remains a popular and affordable collectible. In Good condition, it is worth about $11, in VF-20, about $16, and in MS-60, about $22. Mintage: 27,995,000.

1909—Starting in August 1909, the rest of the year's cents had no initials on the reverse. In Good, these are worth $3.50; in VF-20, about $5; and in MS-60, $17. Mintage: 72,702,618.

1909-S, V.D.B.—Much rarer than the 1909 Philadelphia cents are those minted in San Francisco. The 1909-S, V.D.B., cent is the "key" to the series—the one that every collector searches for! Only 484,000 were minted, and today a Mint State example can be worth thousands of dollars. (Good condition, $825;

1909-S, V.D.B.—the key date in the Lincoln cent series.

VF-20, $1,250; MS-60, $1,700.) It was ranked no. 19 among the *100 Greatest U.S. Coins* (Garrett/Guth). Collectors pay big bucks for high-grade examples; in April 2012 one graded MS-66 was auctioned for more than $12,000.

1909-S—Like their Philadelphia counterparts, some San Francisco cents were also minted without Brenner's initials. The 1909-S cent without initials is uncommon, with only 1,825,000 minted, and is worth hundreds of dollars if Uncirculated. (Good condition, $100; VF-20, $150; MS-60, $325. In higher grades, the coin is even more valuable: in April 2012 a 1909-S cent graded MS-66 sold at auction for $2,185!) The mintmark appears under the date.

(After the coin's first year, did Victor David Brenner ever get to have his initials on the coin again? In fact, he did—they were finally restored in 1918, placed in very small letters on Lincoln's shoulder.)

1910-S, 1911-S, 1912-S, 1913-S, 1914-S, 1915-S—Lincoln cents struck at the San Francisco Mint in the coin's early years are all worth some money— about $15 to $25 in Good condition, $25 to $65 in VF-20, and $100 to $325 or more in Mint State. Look for the S mintmark under the date.

Early-date Lincoln cents minted in San Francisco. Note the S mintmark underneath the date.

1914-D—The 1914-D Lincoln cent is a rarity in any grade, even worn-out Good. Only 1,193,000 cents of 1914 were struck in Denver, compared to more than 75,000,000 in Philadelphia. Collectors didn't realize exactly how rare the 1914-D coin was until the 1930s, when Whitman's (and other companies') coin boards and folders became popular, and people started saving cents from their pocket

1914-D: a valuable key to the series—but one that is sometimes counterfeited, so buy with care.

change. Inevitably the 1914-D would be one of the last holes to be filled. By the time collectors realized how rare the coin was, most examples had been worn down in circulation, to grades such as Fine and Very Fine.

Collectors are careful to make sure their 1914-D cent is genuine, and not a fraudulently altered date or mintmark. One diagnostic: Brenner's initials, V.D.B., do not appear on Lincoln's shoulder on a genuine 1914-D cent. As noted above, the initials were used in 1909, removed, and then returned in 1918.

The ever-popular 1914-D cent in Good condition is worth $215 . . . in VF-20, $475 . . . and in MS-60, $2,000 or more. In April 2012 an example graded MS-64 sold at auction for $7,475.

1922-D—Lincoln cents in 1922 were struck only at the Denver Mint, and all of them are valuable. The regular 1922-D is worth about $20 in Good condition, $27 in VF-20, and $100-plus in Mint State. However, there are two varieties of the 1922-D that are worth even more.

The so-called Weak D was struck from a worn-out obverse die, making the D mintmark barely visible; examples are worth $30 in Good condition, $80 in VF-20, and $400 or more in Mint State.

The even more valuable 1922-D, No D, cent—sometimes called "Plain"—was struck from a worn obverse die that a Mint technician tinkered with to reduce its surface roughness and extend the die's life. In the process, he completely ground off the D mintmark. Coins made from the resulting die have no D visible at all. Experts can tell whether a 1922-D, No D, cent was genuinely struck from that particular die, or if a fraudster took a regular 1922-D (or a Weak D) and buffed away the mintmark. A genuine No D is worth $750 in Good condition, $1,650 in VF-20, and $11,000 or more in Mint State! An example in AU-58 condition (nearly Mint State) sold for $5,463 in an April 2012 auction.

1922-D, regular strike.   1922-D, Weak D.   1922-D, No D ("Plain").

1924-D—The Lincoln cent was minted in Philadelphia, Denver, and San Francisco in 1924. Of the three, the 1924-D is the most valuable, bringing $40 in Good condition, $60 in VF-20, and $320 or more in MS-60. Coins kept in pristine condition are worth a pretty penny—in April 2012 a 1924-D graded MS-64 was auctioned for $3,738.

The 1924-D had the lowest Lincoln cent mintage since the 1914-D, making it a semi-key issue in the series. Collectors saved many of them from pocket change in the 1930s.

1926-S—The 1926-S Lincoln cent is worth $9 in Good condition, $17 in VF-20, and $85 or more in Mint State. Higher grades can be very valuable: in April 2012 an MS-64 example sold for $12,075 at auction!

Q. David Bowers, in *A Guide Book of Lincoln Cents,* noted that "The low mintage [of the 1926-S] has hallmarked this as a key issue ever since collectors began plucking coins from circulation in the 1930s."

1931-S—Only 866,000 cents were minted in San Francisco in 1931, making them a key to the series. Most of the coins were held by the Treasury in 1931, instead of being widely released. Later, some were made available to collectors and investors at face value. As a result, half or more of the mintage has been saved in Mint State, and a high-grade example can be purchased for less than twice the cost of a well-circulated coin. In Good condition, the 1931-S is worth $110; in VF-20, $135; and in MS-60, $175. In April 2012 an MS-66 example sold for $1,495 at auction.

A low mintage—fewer than a million coins!—makes the 1931-S a famous key in the Lincoln cent series.

1936, Doubled-Die Obverse—Some cents of 1936 show doubling in the date and the legends. These are scarcer than the regular 1936 (which is fairly common). In Fine condition, they are worth $25 apiece; in VF-20, about $50; and in MS-60, about $170. Of course, there's no telling what price an unusual variety will bring at auction (when the right bidders are battling for the right coin in a perfect storm); in April 2012 a 1936, Doubled-Die Obverse, sold for $173 in VF-30 condition.

1936, Doubled-Die Obverse. Several variations exist.

1943—Copper was strategic to the nation's war effort during World War II. To help conserve the metal, the Treasury Department switched the Lincoln cent from bronze (made of 95% copper) to zinc-coated steel. This change was in effect only for a single year—1943—but it helped save millions of pounds of copper for military use.

Steel cents were minted in Philadelphia, Denver, and San Francisco in 1943.

No bronze cents were officially issued in 1943, but a few specimens struck by error on bronze or silver planchets are known to exist. The famous bronze 1943 cent was ranked no. 4 among the *100 Greatest U.S. Error Coins* (Brown/Camire/Weinberg), and examples have sold for more than $100,000 in recent years. (Beware the many regular steel cents of 1943 that were later plated with copper, either as dime-store novelties or to deceive collectors. A quick test for authenticity is to hold a magnet next to the coin; if it looks bronze but it sticks to the magnet, it's steel.)

Steel cents were minted by the hundreds of millions, so they're not particularly scarce today, being worth $0.10 to $0.50 apiece in circulated grades, $3 to $6 in MS-63, and $8 to $20 in MS-65, depending on the mint.

1944–1946—From 1944 to 1946, scrap military-ammunition cases were salvaged and mixed with copper to make into Lincoln cents. Technically, the new alloy was brass and not bronze, since it contained no tin (just copper and zinc). In Mint State grades, the Lincoln cents of these years have a slightly different color than earlier bronze examples.

Billions of cents were minted from 1944 through 1946, making them fairly common. Values range from $0.10 to $0.75 or so in Very Fine condition to Mint State. Beyond their collector value, the coins are significant for their history and their connection to World War II.

The brass "cartridge-shell" cents of 1944 to 1946 were made at all three mints: Philadelphia, Denver, and San Francisco.

A few 1944 cents were accidentally struck on steel planchets from 1943. If you have a 1944 cent that appears to be steel but isn't attracted to a magnet, it's a plated novelty.

1955, Doubled-Die Obverse—The popular and famous 1955 doubled-die cents are error coins made from improperly prepared dies. They show a fully doubled outline of the date and legends. Q. David Bowers, in the *Guide Book of Lincoln Cents*, describes how they came to be: "I inquired at the Philadelphia Mint and learned that, on a particular day in 1955, several presses were coining cents, dumping the cents into a box where they were then collected and mixed with the cents from other coining presses. Late in the afternoon, a Mint inspector noticed the bizarre doubled cents and removed the offending die. By that time, somewhat more than 40,000 cents had been produced, about

The 1955 Doubled Die Obverse cent—a famous and valuable error coin. Check your rolls of Wheat cents!

24,000 of which had been mixed with normal cents from other presses. The decision was made to destroy the cents still in the box, and to release into circulation the 24,000 or so pieces which were mixed with other cents. The Mint had no reason to believe that these would attract attention or have value with collectors. They were simply viewed as defective coins." Bowers estimates that 3,000 to 4,000 of the coins have survived over the years. If you find one, you're in for a treat: collectors pay about $1,750 in Very Fine condition, up to $3,500 or so in MS-63—and they've been known to go for $50,000-plus in MS-65.

As with other valuable key dates, many counterfeits exist of the 1955 Doubled-Die Obverse cent. In genuine examples, the reverse die is misaligned about 5 percent from the normal 180-degree rotation.

Proofs—The U.S. Mint made Proof Wheat cents from 1909 to 1916, then in various years in the 1930s and 1940s, and every year from 1950 to 1958. Later Proofs are inexpensive, worth about $10 or $20 up to $100 or so in higher Proof levels such as PF-67 with full red luster. Proofs before 1952 can be worth hundreds or even thousands of dollars. In October 2011 a PF-64 1909, V.D.B., cent sold at auction for $23,000!

LINCOLN CENTS, MEMORIAL REVERSE
(1959–2008)

The Lincoln cent got a new reverse design in 1959, on the 150th anniversary of Abraham Lincoln's birth: a view of the Lincoln Memorial in Washington, D.C. The motif was designed by Mint artist Frank Gasparro, who would later become chief engraver. The coin went through several changes in composition over the years; first in 1962, when tin was eliminated from the copper alloy, and then in 1982 when it was changed to copper-plated zinc. Other changes over time included modifications of the dies to strengthen the designs, and to enlarge or

Copper alloy (1959–1982).

Copper-plated zinc (1982–2008).

reduce various elements like the engraver's initials (FG), Lincoln's bust, the lettering, and the date.

Proofs were struck for most years, for collectors.

Most Lincoln Memorial cents will cost you only $0.01 to collect. A complete collection of basic dates and mintmarks can be assembled from circulation, by searching rolls from local banks or stores, and, for more elusive pieces, by looking through the inventory of your local coin shop.

As with the earlier Wheat cents, there are several popular and valuable varieties among the Lincoln Memorial cents.

1960, Small Date—Two sizes of dates were used on the Lincoln cent in 1960 (for coins struck in both Philadelphia and Denver). The less common variety is the 1960 Small Date, which is worth $3 in MS-63, $7 in MS-65, and $38 in MS-66.

Here's how to quickly tell the difference between the Large Date and the Small Date: check the alignment of the 1 and the 9. In the Large Date, the top of the 1 is significantly lower than the top of the 9. In the Small Date, the tops are at the same level.

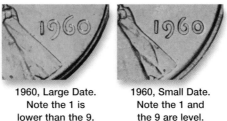

1960, Large Date.
Note the 1 is
lower than the 9.

1960, Small Date.
Note the 1 and
the 9 are level.

1960-D, D Over D, Large Over Small Date—This variety has two die anomalies: the mintmark is doubled ("D Over D"), and the date is actually a Large Date over a Small Date. These features appear as repetitions of the mintmark and 1960. This unusual coin can be worth $200 to $500 in Mint State up to MS-65, and $2,000 or more in higher grades. In August 2011 an example graded MS-64 was auctioned for $293.

1960, D Over D, Large
Over Small Date.

1969-S, Doubled-Die Obverse—When is 3 grams of copper and zinc worth $50,000 to $75,000 or more? When it's in the form of a 1969-S Lincoln cent with a doubled-die obverse! An example of this rare variety, graded MS-64, sold at auction in February 2012 for $80,500.

1969-S, Doubled-Die Obverse.

1970-S, Small Date (High 7)—Check your 1970-S cents for the uncommon Small Date variety. A quick diagnostic to check is the 7 in relation to the 0 in the date. On the Small Date variety, the top of the 7 is high; on the Large Date, the 0 is higher than the 7. This coin can be worth $25 in MS-63, $55 in MS-65, and $240 in MS-66.

1970-S, Small Date   1970-S, Large Date
(High 7).   (Low 7).

1972, Doubled-Die Obverse—Collectors have found yet another doubled die, this one for the 1972 Lincoln cent. It's visually dramatic in its doubling; if you're looking at a 1972 cent and feel like you've been hit over the head, you've got yourself a 1972 DDO—and depending on the grade it's worth about $400 (in MS-63), $625 (MS-65), $1,050 (MS-66), or $5,800 (MS-67). In August 2011 an MS-66 example sold at auction for $920. Be careful, though: several less dramatically doubled varieties exist; they're worth more than a normal coin but much less than the variety pictured here. Also, counterfeits of the 1972 Doubled-Die Obverse are frequently encountered. If you want to buy one, make sure you deal with an experienced, professional numismatist. (This is good advice when you purchase any expensive coin.)

1972, Doubled-Die Obverse. Other less
obvious doubled dies exist for this date.

1983, Doubled-Die Reverse—Another doubled die, this time the reverse, shows up on some 1983 cents. All of the reverse lettering is doubled, as are the designer's initials and portions of the Lincoln Memorial. This scarce variety is worth looking for; in MS-63 it's worth $250; in MS-65, $385; in MS-66, $535; and if you're fortunate enough to find a nearly pristine example in MS-67, it's worth $1,350.

1983, Doubled-Die Reverse.

1990, Proof, No S—If you have any 1990 Proof sets, check the Lincoln cent. It's a long shot, but an estimated 100 to 250 of them were struck without the usual S mintmark (for San Francisco)—probably from a circulation-strike die that had been given a mirror finish and put into service for Proof production. As noted in the *Guide Book of United States Coins, Professional Edition*, "This error escaped the notice of at least 14 people during die preparation and coining." Their mistake could be your profit: a "No S" 1990 Proof cent is worth $4,000 to $5,000 or more, depending on its quality. This die variety was ranked among the *100 Greatest U.S. Modern Coins*.

1990, Proof, No S. Normally the mintmark would be underneath the date.

1990s and 2000, "Wide AM" varieties—In 1992, 1996, 1998, 1999, and 2000, a number of otherwise normal cents were made using dies that were intended for Proof coins. The Proof dies have a wide space between the A and the M in AMERICA. In the normal circulation-strike dies, the letters nearly touch. The Wide AM varieties are scarce, and marketplace values aren't firmly established yet, but collectors do pay more for them. The 1998, Wide AM, is worth $25 in MS-65; the 1999, Wide AM, is worth $500; and the 2000, Wide AM, is worth $20. These coins prove the adage that "knowledge is power"—and can also be cash in your pocket, if you know what to look for.

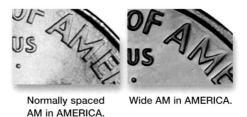

Normally spaced AM in AMERICA.   Wide AM in AMERICA.

1995, Doubled-Die Obverse—Another popularly collected doubled die occurred in 1995. Nearly 30,000 of these coins have been certified by the major third-party grading firms, which is plenty of incentive to look for more—especially when you know their value to collectors: $35 in MS-63; $46 in MS-65; $90 in MS-66; $220 in MS-67. In April 2012 an example graded MS-69 (nearly perfect condition) sold at auction for $1,610—not bad for a coin that started life worth $0.01!

1995, Doubled-Die Obverse.

LINCOLN CENTS, BICENTENNIAL
(2009)

In 2009 the cent got a remake, in the form of four new reverse designs paying unique tribute to President Abraham Lincoln. The coins celebrate the bicentennial of his birth and the 100th anniversary of the debut of the Lincoln cent. Each design represents a major aspect or period of Lincoln's life. For general circulation, they were issued in large quantities (an average of about 300 million coins per mint—Denver and Philadelphia—for each design). However, the coins were released slowly and erratically into commerce, and the mintage for each mint/design on average is only 1/10th that of recent years, so the 2009 Bicentennial cents may seem to be "rarer" than other dates. For example, compare these mintages for Denver cents:

2005-D	3,764,450,500
2007-D	3,638,800,000
2009-D, Birth and Early Childhood	350,400,000
2009-D, Formative Years	363,600,000
2009-D, Professional Life	336,000,000
2009-D, Presidency	198,000,000

Even with their relatively low mintages, a quantity of 300 million coins is plenty to keep any given 2009 cent's value at $0.01 unless its grade is exceptional. A coin dealer who's taken the time to place one into a 2x2 Mylar® holder, staple it shut, and write its date, variety, and grade on the holder might charge $0.15 or $0.25 for his time, effort, and overhead. For the thrill of the hunt, though, you'll get more fun out of searching for the coins in pocket change and building a collection of attractive specimens for face value.

Lincoln's Birth and Early Childhood. The scene is the log cabin in Kentucky where young Abe was born and spent his childhood years.

Lincoln's Formative Years. Representing the Indiana years of 1816 to 1830, this design shows Lincoln sitting on a log, taking a break from rail splitting, reading a book to further his education.

Lincoln's Professional Life. This scene shows Lincoln standing before the State Capitol building in Illinois, where his professional life as an attorney and legislator began.

Lincoln's Presidency. A view of the under-construction U.S. Capitol Dome, which neared completion in 1865, symbolizes Lincoln's work as president, rebuilding the torn-apart nation.

Lincoln Bicentennial Cents
1809–2009

Obverse

Birth and Early Childhood, Kentucky

Formative Years, Indiana

Professional Life, Illinois

Presidency, Washington, DC

"With malice toward none, with charity for all"

2009 Lincoln Bicentennial cents make an attractive and historical collection—a panorama of the martyred president's life in sculpted zinc and copper.

LINCOLN CENTS, SHIELD REVERSE
(2010 TO DATE)

In 2009 the Lincoln Bicentennial cents told the president's life story in four symbolic vignettes. Since 2010, the one-cent coin has featured a shield design "emblematic of President Lincoln's preservation of the United States as a single and united country." In addition the coin has a modern update of Victor David Brenner's original presidential portrait used on the 1909 Lincoln cent.

Lincoln, Shield Reverse, cent.

Mintages are averaging about 4 billion coins per year, split fairly evenly between the Philadelphia and Denver mints (with additional Proofs struck in San Francisco, for collectors). The coins are readily available in the marketplace, and can be collected from circulation for face value.

9
TWO-CENT PIECES

The two-cent piece, like the bronze version of the Indian Head cent, was a byproduct of the American Civil War. The denomination was created in the same legislation (the Mint Act of April 22, 1864) that changed the weight and metallic composition of the one-cent piece.

The two-cent piece is a bronze coin about the same diameter as a quarter. It has a plain edge, like the cent and the nickel (rather than a reeded edge, like the dime, quarter, half dollar, and silver dollar). The motto IN GOD WE TRUST appeared for the first time on the new coin, with the personal support and approval of Treasury Secretary Salmon P. Chase. The coin's design is simple but dignified, with a shield, arrows, and wreath on the obverse (similar to that on the nickel five-cent piece that would be introduced in 1866, just after the Civil War), and on the reverse a wreath with the denomination and UNITED STATES OF AMERICA.

The following is an overview of two-cent pieces. For more detailed information, including values for every date and more grades, consult the *Guide Book of United States Coins* (the "Red Book").

These are prices you'll typically see in coin shops for the most common dates of two-cent pieces, in various conditions.

TWO-CENT PIECES	G-4	F-12	EF-40	MS-60	MS-63	MS-65	PF-63	PF-65
1864–1873	$19	$28	$50	$100	$160	$600	$450	$1,200

TWO-CENT PIECES
(1864–1873)

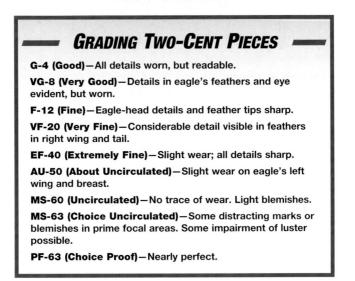

━━━ GRADING TWO-CENT PIECES ━━━

G-4 (Good)—All details worn, but readable.

VG-8 (Very Good)—Details in eagle's feathers and eye evident, but worn.

F-12 (Fine)—Eagle-head details and feather tips sharp.

VF-20 (Very Fine)—Considerable detail visible in feathers in right wing and tail.

EF-40 (Extremely Fine)—Slight wear; all details sharp.

AU-50 (About Uncirculated)—Slight wear on eagle's left wing and breast.

MS-60 (Uncirculated)—No trace of wear. Light blemishes.

MS-63 (Choice Uncirculated)—Some distracting marks or blemishes in prime focal areas. Some impairment of luster possible.

PF-63 (Choice Proof)—Nearly perfect.

The following illustrations show what a Good, Very Fine, and Mint State two-cent piece looks like.

G-6 two-cent piece (shown enlarged).

VF-20 two-cent piece (shown enlarged).

MS-65 two-cent piece (shown enlarged).

The two-cent piece was one of the shortest-lived issues of United States coinage. The coins were struck in the millions in the first two years of issue, while the Civil War was still raging. Coins of all kinds were scarce in circulation in those uncertain times—Americans hoarded their "hard money" (even if it was only bronze, instead of silver or gold), fearful of how the war might end and not trusting the long-term value of paper money. Eventually Indian Head cents began to circulate again (in their new bronze format), in mid-1864 and beyond, and another coin, the nickel three-cent piece, was introduced in 1865. These factors took some pressure off the two-cent piece as a workhorse of commerce, and led the Treasury to lower the mintage dramatically in 1866. Beyond that year continually decreasing quantities were struck, until 1872, the final year of regular coinage, when only 65,000 were made. In 1873 a few hundred examples were minted in Proof format for collectors, and then the series ended with passage of the Coinage Act of 1873.

These unusual little coins are hands-on mementos of the Civil War and Reconstruction era. Most are worth $19 to $32 in Good condition, $28 to $85 in Fine, and $100 to $300 in MS-60. There are two varieties of the 1864 issue: Small Motto and Large Motto. The Small Motto is scarcer, and worth $175 in Good, $450 in VF-20, and $1,200 in MS-60.

1864, Large Motto. The more common of two 1864 varieties, this coin is worth $28 in Fine condition . . . $50 in EF-40 . . . $160 in MS-63.

1864, Small Motto. This variety, scarcer than the Large Motto, is worth $335 in Fine condition . . . $650 in EF-40 . . . $1,500 in MS-63.

10 THREE-CENT PIECES

The three-cent denomination includes the smallest (in terms of size) U.S. coin: the tiny silver trime, minted from 1851 to 1873 and measuring a scant 14 mm in diameter—a bit larger than a half inch. "A set of circulated coins can be gathered through and including 1862," says the *Guide Book of United States Coins, Professional Edition*, "after which such pieces become very rare. Most later dates will have to be acquired on a catch-as-catch-can basis, perhaps by acquiring impaired Proofs for certain of the years."

Three-cent pieces were also minted in a copper-nickel type, 1865 to 1889. "A set of Mint State coins is considerably more difficult than a run of Proofs," according to the *Professional Edition*. "A hand-selected set of well-struck coins MS-65 or finer could take several years to complete."

Of course, collectors can also search for nice circulated examples of each type, building a fine collection of these historic little coins on a much smaller budget.

In the 1850s and 1860s, it cost 3¢ to mail a letter. One silver trime would have paid the rate conveniently.

These are prices you'll typically see in coin shops for the most common dates of silver three-cent pieces (trimes), in various conditions.

THREE-CENT PIECES	G-4	F-12	EF-40	MS-60	MS-63	MS-65	PF-63	PF-65
Silver, Variety 1, 1851–1853	$25	$45	$80	$175	$275	$950	—	—
Silver, Variety 2, 1854–1858	25	45	120	360	675	2,750	$2,750	$7,500
Silver, Variety 3, 1859–1873	25	45	90	215	285	1,000	650	1,500
Copper-Nickel, 1865–1889	18	24	40	125	160	600	350	700

SILVER THREE-CENT PIECES (TRIMES)
(1851–1873)

In 1849 and 1850, after the California Gold Rush started, there was so much gold flooding the nation's commerce that *silver* became disproportionately valuable. The situation was so extreme that it cost the U.S. Mint more to strike silver coins than their face value! As a result, Americans started hoarding the dimes, quarters, and other silver coins they received in change. In order to provide a small silver coin for everyday transactions, Congress enacted a new denomination: the three-cent piece, called a *trime*. But how to discourage people from hoarding the new coins and melting them for their silver? The Mint's solution was to make the trimes only .750 fine, instead of the normal .900, and with less than 3¢ worth of silver each. The resulting coins were very small, only 14 mm in diameter, and weighed less than a gram. The Philadelphia and New Orleans mints were kept busy producing more than 36 million of the tiny coins in 1851, 1852, and 1853.

Trime (silver three-cent piece), shown at actual size.

Minor design modifications were made over the years, mainly in the number of lines outlining the star on the obverse.

When the Mint adjusted downward the amount of silver in its half dimes, dimes, quarters, and half dollars in 1853, public demand for the trime also decreased. The larger coins' face values were once again greater than their precious-metal values, and the public stopped hoarding them, making the trime redundant. The Mint adjusted its production accordingly. By the close of the

1850s only a few hundred thousand were being struck each year, and late in the Civil War annual mintages decreased to 21,000 (1863), 12,000 (1864), and 8,000 (1865) . . . down to only 1,000 coins in 1872, and about 600 (Proofs only; none struck for circulation) in 1873. The latter proved to be the trime's final year. The coin was discontinued under the Coinage Act of 1873, and the Mint melted nearly all of the non-Proof coins it had struck between 1863 and 1872.

Trime (silver three-cent piece), Variety 1,
(1851–1853). Shown 2x actual size.

Trime (silver three-cent piece), Variety 2
(1854–1858). Shown 2x actual size.

Trime (silver three-cent piece), Variety 3
(1859–1873). Shown 2x actual size.

The following illustrations show what Good, Very Fine, and Mint State silver three-cent pieces (trimes) look like.

G-4 silver three-cent piece (shown enlarged).

G-4 (Good)—The star is worn smooth. The legend and date are readable.

VG-8 (Very Good)—The outline of the shield is defined. The legend and date are clear.

F-12 (Fine)—Most of the obverse star's relief is worn. The reverse stars are flat.

VF-20 (Very Fine)—Only partial wear is on the star ridges.

EF-40 (Extremely Fine)—The ridges on the star points (for coins of 1854 onward) are visible.

AU-50 (About Uncirculated)—Traces of wear are visible at each star point. The center of the shield might be weak.

MS-60 (Uncirculated)—No trace of wear. Light blemishes.

MS-63 (Choice Uncirculated)—Some distracting marks or blemishes in prime focal areas. Some impairment of luster is possible.

PF-63 (Choice Proof)—Nearly perfect. Attractive fields. Minimal hairlines. Only a few blemishes in secondary focal areas.

VF-20 silver three-cent piece (shown enlarged).

MS-66 silver three-cent piece (shown enlarged).

Every silver three-cent coin is worth some money—collectors value them *far more* than for their minuscule precious-metal content. (If you look only at their bullion value, with 217 thousandths of an ounce of pure silver, a Variety 2 or Variety 3 trime would be worth about 75¢ when silver hits $35/ounce!) To a collector, any silver trime is worth at least $25 in Good condition, $45 in Very

Fine, or $175 to $275 or more in Mint State. Those dating from 1863 to 1873 are much scarcer, and worth $325 in Good, $375 in Very Fine, or $650 to $1,000 or more in Mint State.

COPPER-NICKEL THREE-CENT PIECES
(1865–1889)

In 1865 Congress had authorized a *copper-nickel* version of the three-cent piece, to boost the number of coins in circulation. (With the Civil War going full-steam, Americans were once again hoarding silver and gold coins, not trusting the future value of U.S. paper currency.) The nickel three-cent piece joined the Indian Head cent and the two-cent piece as a popular small-change coin, and the Mint produced millions of them for commerce. When a nickel *five-cent* coin was introduced in 1866, demand for the three-cent piece

Nickel three-cent piece, shown at actual size.

Nickel three-cent piece (1865–1889). Shown 2x actual size.

started to decline. Mintages ramped down as a result, although the coin held on until the late 1880s, by which time only a few thousand were being minted annually.

The following illustrations show what Good, Very Fine, and Mint State copper-nickel three-cent pieces look like.

G-4 copper-nickel three-cent piece (shown enlarged).

G-4 (Good)—The date and legends are complete, though worn. Numeral III is smooth.

VG-8 (Very Good)—III is half worn. The rims are complete.

F-12 (Fine)—The forehead blends into the hair above it. Many vertical lines in III are worn together. The denticles are distinct.

VF-20 (Very Fine)—Three-quarters of the hair details are visible.

EF-40 (Extremely Fine)—Slight, even wear.

AU-50 (About Uncirculated)—Slight wear on hair curls, above the forehead, and on the wreath and III.

MS-60 (Uncirculated)—No trace of wear. Light blemishes.

MS-63 (Choice Uncirculated)—Some distracting marks or blemishes in prime focal areas. Some impairment of luster is possible.

PF-63 (Choice Proof)—Nearly perfect. Attractive fields. Minimal hairlines. Only a few blemishes in secondary focal areas.

VF-20 copper-nickel three-cent piece (shown enlarged).

MS-65 copper-nickel three-cent piece (shown enlarged).

Like their silver cousins, copper-nickel three-cent pieces are valuable, as well. Collectors pay $18 in Good condition for a common date, $28 in VF-20, or $125 in MS-60. Scarcer dates are those from 1879, 1880, and 1882 to 1889; these range from $60–$410 in Good condition (depending on the date), $90–$575 in VF-20, and $300–$950 in MS-60.

11
NICKEL FIVE-CENT PIECES

The copper-nickel five-cent piece, which everybody today just calls a *nickel*, didn't exist for the first 90 years of our nation. There was a *silver* five-cent coin, which had been around since the early days of the Philadelphia Mint in the 1790s, but the 75% copper, 25% nickel version didn't debut until 1866, a year after the Civil War ended.

America's nickels are very popular with coin collectors. The denomination includes some great American classics (who hasn't heard of the Buffalo nickel?), famous rarities (like the 1913 Liberty Head), and innovative new designs (like the Westward Journey series). Folders, albums, display cases, and other supplies are available to help you build your collection. It's not silver, it's not gold—but the humble nickel is indeed a coin to be treasured.

For several generations of Americans all it took to buy a refreshing bottle of Coca-Cola was a five-cent nickel.

These are prices you'll typically see for the most common dates of each major type of nickel, in various conditions.

FIVE-CENT PIECES	G-4	F-12	EF-40	MS-60	MS-63	MS-65	PF-63	PF-65
Shield, Rays, 1866–1867	$28.00	$50.00	$170.00	$275	$425	$2,400	$2,250	$3,500
Shield, No Rays, 1867–1883	20.00	25.00	60.00	140	225	800	385	650
Liberty Head, No CENTS, 1883	7.00	8.00	12.00	35	50	225	250	700
Liberty Head, CENTS, 1883–1912	1.75	4.25	30.00	70	125	500	250	700
Buffalo, Variety 1, 1913	11.00	16.00	25.00	45	60	170	1,200	3,250
Buffalo, Variety 2, 1913–1938	0.50	1.75	3.00	22	36	60	1,000	2,250
Jefferson, War (Silver), 1942–1945	Bullion	Bullion	2.25	6	9	20	200	225

SHIELD NICKELS
(1866–1883)

In the mid-1860s no silver or gold coins were circulating in the East or the Midwest; people hoarded them and instead spent small-change coins and various kinds of paper currency. The coins passing hands in those days were Indian Head cents, bronze two-cent pieces, nickel three-cent coins, and a new animal in the numismatic menagerie—the Shield nickel, brought to life by the Act of May 16, 1866.

Mint engraver James B. Longacre designed the coin, adapting the shield motif he created in 1864 for the two-cent piece. All Shield nickels were struck at the Philadelphia Mint.

Shield nickel, Variety 1, Rays Between Stars (1866–1867).

Shield nickel, Variety 2, Without Rays (1867–1883).

GRADING SHIELD NICKELS

G-4 (Good)—All letters in the motto IN GOD WE TRUST are readable.

VG-8 (Very Good)—The motto is clear and stands out. The rims are slightly worn, but even. Part of the shield lines are visible.

F-12 (Fine)—Half of each olive leaf is worn smooth.

VF-20 (Very Fine)—The shield frame shows some detail, as do the leaves. In the shield stripes, some of the vertical lines blend together.

EF-40 (Extremely Fine)—The leaf tips and the cross over the shield have slight wear.

AU-50 (About Uncirculated)—Traces of light wear are visible only on the high points of the design. Half of the mint luster is present.

MS-60 (Uncirculated)—No trace of wear. Light blemishes.

MS-63 (Choice Uncirculated)—Some distracting marks or blemishes in prime focal areas. Some impairment of luster possible.

PF-63 (Choice Proof)—Nearly perfect.

The following illustrations show what a Good, Very Fine, and Mint State Shield nickel looks like.

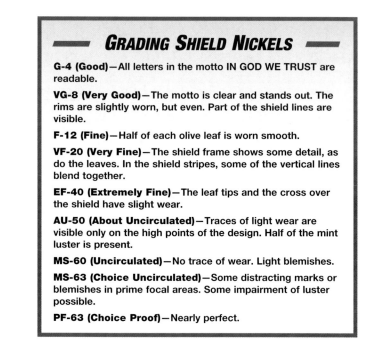

G-4 Shield nickel (shown enlarged).

VF-20 Shield nickel (shown enlarged).

MS-66 Shield nickel (shown enlarged).

Shield nickels can be found in circulated grades, generally in proportion to their mintages, which range from a low of 16,000 (1880) to a high of 28,890,500 (1867, Without Rays). Common dates are worth about $20 in Good condition . . . $60 in EF-40 . . . or $140 in MS-60. The scarcer dates are the 1879, 1880, and 1881, which are worth $250 to $475 even in G-4 condition.

Proofs were made each year and sold by the Mint to collectors. Today most of them are worth from a few hundred to a couple thousand dollars. A notable exception is the 1867, With Rays, Proof—only a couple dozen were minted, and one sold at auction in January 2012 for $109,250!

LIBERTY HEAD NICKELS
(1883–1912)

Early in 1883, the nickel was updated with a new design by Mint engraver Charles E. Barber. A profile portrait of Miss Liberty wearing a tiara is on the obverse, and a large Roman numeral V in a wreath on the reverse.

Liberty Head nickel, Variety 1, Without CENTS (1883).

The first version of the Liberty Head nickel is famous as one of the great mistakes in U.S. coinage. The "V" on the reverse was, of course, symbolic of the denomination—five cents. But the coin didn't have the word CENTS anywhere on it. Normally this wouldn't be confusing; Americans had been using a roughly 21-millimeter copper-nickel five-cent coin for 17 years—there were about three nickels in circulation for every man, woman, and child in the United States in 1883. But clever conmen took advantage of a convenient (for them) little coincidence: the gold five-*dollar* coin in circulation at the time was also about 21 millimeters in diameter.

Liberty Head nickel, Variety 2, With CENTS (1883–1912).

Mintmark is on the reverse, to the left of CENTS.

They plated some of the new Liberty Head nickels with a light gold wash, cut their edges with reeding, and passed them off as new $5 gold pieces. (According to legend, the con would go off like this: A respectable-looking man walks into a shop, selects a 5¢ cigar, plunks down a gold-plated, reeded-edge nickel as payment, and stands there without saying a word, as if expecting his change. The cashier, unfamiliar with the new nickel and assuming it's the latest $5 coin, hands him $4.95. The conman pockets his cigar and his ill-gotten profit—all without having spoken a word of deceit.) Word got back to the Mint about these "racketeer nickels," and later in the year the word CENTS was added to discourage any confusion.

The Liberty Head nickel was minted for circulation for nearly 30 years, from 1883 to 1912, after which it was replaced by the Buffalo nickel. However, in 1913 someone at the Philadelphia Mint secretly made five nickels of the Liberty Head design with a 1913 date. The coins were purchased from a former Mint employee in the 1920s by super-collector Colonel E.H.R. Green (son of the famous Wall Street millionaire Hetty Green, the richest woman in America). Over time the five coins were dispersed. Today one is in the Smithsonian's National Numismatic Collection, one belongs to the American Numismatic Association, and three are held in private collections (with one of those on loan to the ANA's Edward C. Rochette Money Museum, in Colorado Springs).

The famous 1913 Liberty Head nickel— not a regular Mint issue, and never placed in circulation, but made in secret after the series officially ended in 1912. One of the five known examples sold at auction in January 2010 for $3,737,500. (shown enlarged)

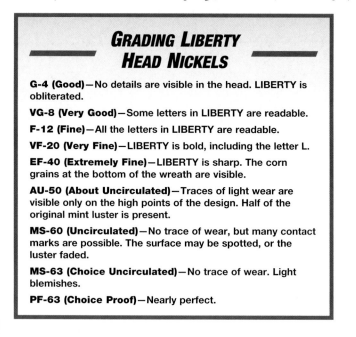

GRADING LIBERTY HEAD NICKELS

G-4 (Good)—No details are visible in the head. LIBERTY is obliterated.

VG-8 (Very Good)—Some letters in LIBERTY are readable.

F-12 (Fine)—All the letters in LIBERTY are readable.

VF-20 (Very Fine)—LIBERTY is bold, including the letter L.

EF-40 (Extremely Fine)—LIBERTY is sharp. The corn grains at the bottom of the wreath are visible.

AU-50 (About Uncirculated)—Traces of light wear are visible only on the high points of the design. Half of the original mint luster is present.

MS-60 (Uncirculated)—No trace of wear, but many contact marks are possible. The surface may be spotted, or the luster faded.

MS-63 (Choice Uncirculated)—No trace of wear. Light blemishes.

PF-63 (Choice Proof)—Nearly perfect.

The following illustrations show what a Good, Very Fine, and Mint State Liberty Head nickel looks like.

G-4 Liberty Head nickel (shown enlarged).

VF-20 Liberty Head nickel (shown enlarged).

MS-64 Liberty Head nickel (shown enlarged).

Liberty Head nickels were struck in large quantities in most years (at the Philadelphia Mint through 1912, with Denver and San Francisco also minting the coins in that final year). The nickels were popular in American commerce in their time, and continued to circulate in day-to-day transactions into the 1940s. By that time most Liberty Head nickels found in pocket change were worn down to Good condition or so. In the 1930s, when Whitman and other hobby publishers made coin boards a popular pastime, collectors began pulling the nickels out of circulation, looking for one of each date and mintmark to complete their collections. Many of the scarcer dates were plucked out of change during those years.

Today a common-date Liberty Head nickel in Good condition is worth about $1.75 . . . in VF-20, about $13 . . . and in MS-60, about $70. Slightly more valuable dates include the 1883, With CENTS variety (worth $55 in VF-20), the 1888 ($120 in VF-20), the 1894 ($165 in VF-20), and the 1912-D ($38 in

VF-20). Many Americans saved the 1883, Without CENTS, variety as a novel keepsake in the coin's debut year, and kept them tucked away in desk drawers and other safe places; as a result, the 1883 Without CENTS is fairly common in beautiful, lustrous Mint State (in MS-63, the coin is worth a relatively low $50). Scarcer dates to look for include the 1885, 1886, and 1912-S (each worth hundreds of dollars in circulated grades, and thousands in Mint State).

Proofs were made each year and sold by the Mint to collectors. Today most of them are worth a few hundred dollars in PF-63.

BUFFALO OR INDIAN HEAD NICKELS
(1913–1938)

The Mint debuted a new design on the nickel five-cent coin in 1913. It would quickly be hailed as a great U.S. classic—a combination of distinctly American themes, boldly rendered by the talented hand of sculptor James Earle Fraser. On the front was the strong and noble profile of a Native American; on the back, the solid and impressive "monarch of the Great Plains," an American bison. From this animal the coin would derive its popular name as the Buffalo nickel.

Buffalo nickel,
Variety 1 (1913).

FIVE CENTS on raised ground.

Buffalo nickel,
Variety 2 (1913–1938).

FIVE CENTS in recess.

The following illustrations show what a Good, Very Fine, and Mint State Buffalo nickel looks like.

G-4 Buffalo nickel (shown enlarged).

GRADING BUFFALO NICKELS

G-4 (Good)—The legends and date are readable. The bison's horn does not show.

VG-8 (Very Good)—The horn is worn nearly flat.

F-12 (Fine)—The horn and tail are smooth but partially visible. The obverse rim is intact.

VF-20 (Very Fine)—Much of the horn is visible. The Indian's cheekbone is worn.

EF-40 (Extremely Fine)—The horn is lightly worn. Slight wear is seen on the Indian's hair ribbon.

AU-50 (About Uncirculated)—Traces of light wear are visible only on the high points of the design. Half of the original mint luster is present.

MS-60 (Uncirculated)—No trace of wear. May have several blemishes.

MS-63 (Choice Uncirculated)—No trace of wear. Light blemishes.

PF-63 (Choice Proof)—Nearly perfect.

VF-20 Buffalo nickel (shown enlarged).

MS-65 Buffalo nickel (shown enlarged).

Buffalo nickels are available in circulated grades generally in proportion to their mintages. The quantities made of each year/mintmark vary widely—for example, only 970,000 of the 1921-S were struck (and the coin is worth $8,750 in MS-63 today as a result of that scarcity), while nearly 119,000,000 of the 1936 were struck (resulting in an MS-63 value of only $40).

These nickels became popular to collect in the mid-1930s, after Whitman and other hobby firms started making fill-the-hole coin boards, with openings for each date/mint. Collectors could pick Buffalo nickels out of their pocket change well into the 1950s, after which the numismatic herds thinned in the wild. By that time most of them dating from the teens were likely to have their dates worn completely off, or nearly so.

Americans saved the first-year issues of 1913 as novelties, socking them away as souvenirs of the new coin type; Uncirculated examples are relatively common today and are worth perhaps $40 to $90 in lower Mint State grades.

Today common-date circulated Buffalo nickels from the 1930s can be purchased in quantity for about $20–$40 per roll ($0.50 to $1.00 per coin). Prices of $2 to $3 for VF-20 and $22 or so for MS-60 are not uncommon. Their affordability is part of what makes Buffalo nickels so popular with collectors. At the same time, there are many scarcer and more valuable coins in the series. Those from 1913 to 1918 are worth more than many others (for example, the 1915-S is worth $50 in G-4, $200 in VF-20, or $650 in MS-60). From the 1920s and 1930s, look for these dates in particular: 1920-D, 1921-S, 1924-S, 1925-D, 1926-D, 1926-S, and 1931-S.

Matte Proofs (not shiny and mirror-like, but more muted) of 1913 to 1916 are rare. Proofs were also struck in the later teens, the 1920s, and 1930s, mostly in brilliant mirror format.

Several valuable die varieties are worth searching for, too. Here's a small sampling of three of the most popular (for more, see the *Cherrypickers' Guide to Rare Die Varieties*):

1916, Doubled-Die Obverse—The date, chin, throat, feathers, and the tie on the braid are all doubled in this variety. This is a scarce and eagerly sought-after coin—collectors will pay $2,200 in G-4 condition, $11,000 in VF-20, and $60,000 in MS-60. In a November 2007 auction, an MS-64 example sold for $316,250.

1916, Doubled-Die Obverse—
a variety worth more than
1,000 times the value of a
regular 1916 Buffalo nickel!

1918-D, 8 Over 7—In August 2006, an example of this variety graded MS-65 sold at auction for $350,750! The *Cherrypickers' Guide* gives this advice: "Look for the small die crack immediately above the tie on the braid, leading slightly downward to the Indian's jaw. The

1918-D, 8 Over 7.

beginning of this die break can usually be seen even on lower-grade coins." This coin is worth $1,000 in Good condition, $5,500 in VF-20, or $34,000 in MS-60.

1937-D, 3-Legged Buffalo—This famous variety was caused after a reverse die was polished heavily, perhaps to remove damage, resulting in the shaft of the bison's front right leg going missing. Beware of altered specimens fraudulently presented as genuine—look for a line of raised dots from the middle of the bison's belly to the ground, a feature shared by all genuine examples. This variety is worth $550 in Good condition, $900 in VF-20, and $2,500 in MS-60.

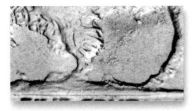

1937-D, 3-Legged Buffalo.

JEFFERSON NICKELS
(1938 TO DATE)

In 1938 the Buffalo nickel had been in circulation for 25 years, which was the statutory minimum period before a U.S. coinage design could be replaced. The coin was a challenge for Mint technicians. They had difficulty in getting it to strike nicely with the full design in strong detail, and struggled to maintain the coinage dies without them breaking under the pressure. The Mint decided it was time for an update.

In early 1938 nearly 400 artists entered a public competition to come up with a new design for the nickel. The subjects were to be a portrait of President Thomas Jefferson and a view of Monticello, his plantation home in Virginia. The April 21 *Washington Post* described the entries: "Jefferson . . . never looked

Monticello reverse (1938–2003).

Wartime silver alloy (1942–1945). The mintmark is above Monticello.

Peace Medal reverse (2004).

Keelboat reverse (2004).

New profile obverse (2005).

American Bison reverse (2005).

Ocean in View reverse (2005).

Three-quarters profile portrait (2006 to date).

Monticello reverse (2006 to date).

like so many different people as he did yesterday. The models depicted him as everything from a coarse barbarian to a royal dandy. The facial features varied from skinny to the triple-chin type. On a few casts, Jefferson scowled. He smiled on none, usually wearing a calm expression. On some models, Jefferson wore his hair in a typical colonial pigtail. On others he had bobbed and even marcelled his hair. The classic Monticello fared little better, the competitors, in some instances, perching eagles on its roof. In violation of rules for the contest, some artists substituted the Liberty Bell and even an ear of corn for the house."

Mint Director Nellie Tayloe Ross and a panel of sculptors judged the entries, and in late April announced the winner: German-born artist Felix Oscar Schlag. After some tweaking of the design (in particular Schlag's rendering of Monticello), the new Jefferson nickel was born. It has been a favorite of U.S. coin collectors ever since, with billions struck for commerce, and high-quality Proofs available for almost every year. Variations in composition, changes in the mintmark and the designer's initials, modification to the designs, and other dynamic factors make the Jefferson nickel a fascinating series to collect and study.

The following illustrations show what a Very Fine, Extremely Fine, and Mint State Jefferson nickel looks like. Because they're so common, collectors most often seek them in Mint State.

VF-20 Jefferson nickel (shown enlarged).

EF-40 Jefferson nickel (shown enlarged).

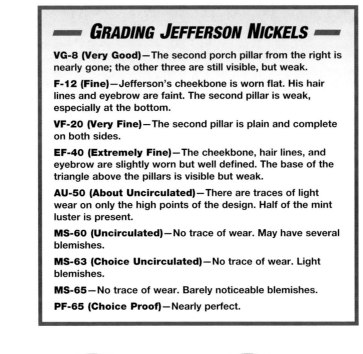

MS-67 Jefferson nickel (shown enlarged).

Collectors and speculators have saved all the basic dates and mintmarks of Jefferson nickels in large quantities, by the roll, since the series started. Scarce issues in Mint State include the 1939-D and the 1942-D.

On October 8, 1942, ten months after the United States entered World War II, a new composition was introduced for the five-cent coin. The alloy of 56% copper, 35% silver, and 9% manganese eliminated *nickel* from the nickel, saving some 2.4 million pounds of the important metal for strategic wartime usage. About 860 million "silver war nickels" were made from 1942 to 1945. A large letter above Monticello indicates where each coin was minted—Philadelphia (with a P), Denver (D), or San Francisco (S). The pre-war composition of 75% copper and 25% nickel was resumed in 1946.

In 1950 the Denver Mint's coinage caused a sensation. The 1950-D nickel was a very popular coin because right from the start collectors knew it had a relatively small mintage: 2,630,030 coins (compared to 36,498,000 for the 1949-D, and 44,734,000 for the 1948-D, for example). Huge numbers of them were hoarded. Today an MS-60 example is worth $14, but in the early 1960s, at the height of wild speculation and an overactive market in rolls and bags of the coins, a single 1950-D nickel was worth up to $30—that's in 1964 dollars, the equivalent

The 1950-D Jefferson nickel was selling for $1,200 a roll (40 coins) in 1964, at the height of a manic investor frenzy.

of $219 today! Ironically, today this "rarity" is one of the most common dates in Mint State, and it's harder to find a *circulated* example of the coin.

The Westward Journey series of nickels (2004–2006) commemorated the bicentennial of the Louisiana Purchase and the journey of Meriwether Lewis and William Clark to explore that vast territory. They feature several new obverse and reverse designs for the nickel. (Thomas Jefferson was president when Louisiana was purchased from the French, hugely increasing the size of the United States.)

Many Jefferson nickels, even older dates, can still be picked from circulation and collected in a Whitman blue folder or coin album. Popular and valuable die varieties are worth searching for, too. You'll find many of them listed in the *Cherrypickers' Guide to Rare Die Varieties.* Here's a sampling:

1939, Doubled-Die Reverse—Very strong doubling is evident to the right of the primary letters, most noticeably on MON-TICELLO and FIVE CENTS. This variety is worth $75 in VF-20 . . . $175 in MS-60 . . . and $1,000 in MS-65.

1939, Doubled-Die Reverse.

1942-D, D Over Horizontal D—The initial D mintmark was punched into the die horizontally instead of vertically, and then corrected. According to the *Cherrypickers' Guide,* "This is the rarest of the major Jefferson nickel varieties in Mint State." If you find one, it can be worth a fancy dinner or a nice used car, depending on the grade: collectors pay $75 in VF-20 condition, $500 in AU-50, and up to $3,000 in MS-60, with experts speculating that an MS-65 example would bring $10,000 at auction.

1942-D, D Over Horizontal D.

1971-S, No S—Check your 1971 Proof sets; a few 1971 Proof nickels were accidentally made without the standard S mintmark for San Francisco. Expect a tidy windfall if you find one: they're worth $1,000 in PF-65, and several thousand dollars in PF-69.

12

HALF DIMES

The Mint Act of April 2, 1792, provided for a silver five-cent coin. The first examples were called *half dismes* (spelled with an *s* but likely pronounced the same as "dime"), and about 1,500 of them were minted in 1792. These first-year-of-issue coins are very rare and expensive today, with an estimated 200 and 300 pieces surviving. After that, half dimes were minted with designs ranging from the Flowing Hair (1794–1795) to various Liberty Seated motifs (late 1830s to early 1870s), similar to the designs used on dimes, quarters, and half dollars of the same years. Half dime mintages varied from year to year, from lows of several thousand to highs of more than 13 million (in 1853). The coins are very small and require a magnifying glass to be studied. Enough types and varieties exist to make them a fun and challenging denomination to collect.

Christian Gobrecht was the engraver of the Liberty Seated half dime obverse.

1792 half disme.

Flowing Hair half dime (1794–1795).

Draped Bust half dime,
Small Eagle Reverse
(1796–1797).

Draped Bust half dime,
Heraldic Eagle Reverse
(1800–1805).

Capped Bust half dime
(1829–1837).

Liberty Seated half dime,
Variety 1, No Stars on
Obverse (1837–1838).

Liberty Seated half dime,
Variety 2, Stars on Obverse
(1838–1853 and 1856–1859).

Liberty Seated half dime,
Variety 3, Arrows at Date
(1853–1855).

Liberty Seated half dime,
Variety 4, Legend on
Obverse (1860–1873).

TYPICAL VALUES FOR HALF DIMES

Many later-date half dimes from the 1830s on can be collected for less than $100 apiece in nice EF-40 condition. The denomination also includes some rarities worth thousands of dollars in higher circulated grades. Mint State examples are available in the marketplace. The Flowing Hair and Draped Bust types are the most valuable.

This chart shows prices you'll typically see for the most common dates of each major type of half dime, in various conditions. For more detailed pricing by date, see the *Guide Book of United States Coins.*

HALF DIMES	G-4	F-12	EF-40	MS-60	MS-63	MS-65	PF-63	PF-65
Flowing Hair, 1794–1795	$1,200	$1,850	$5,000	$13,500	$20,000	$40,000	—	—
Draped Bust, Small Eagle, 1796–1797	1,200	2,250	7,500	15,250	25,000	80,000	$2,750	$7,500
Draped Bust, Heraldic Eagle, 1800–1805	725	1,750	5,750	12,500	20,000	47,500	650	1,500
Capped Bust, 1829–1837	45	75	165	375	850	2,850	10,000	35,000
Liberty Seated, No Stars, 1837–1838	40	80	235	750	1,100	3,000	14,000	37,500
Liberty Seated, With Stars, 1838–1859	16	27	75	210	325	1,200	12,000	26,000
Liberty Seated, With Arrows, 1853–1855	18	24	65	210	310	1,500	8,500	14,000
Liberty Seated, With Legend, 1860–1873	16	25	45	150	275	800	575	1,750

GRADING HALF DIMES

See the chapter on dimes for instructions on grading similarly designed half dimes.

13

DIMES

The dime has been a standard U.S. coin since the late 1790s. The denomination has featured many interesting designs over the years, and all are popular with collectors. Specialists carefully study the details of early varieties, spending hundreds and even thousands of dollars to upgrade their collections; meanwhile, later-date Roosevelt dimes are common enough that a beautiful collection can be assembled from pocket change, for face value. Adding to their allure, dimes were made of good old-fashioned American silver up into the early 1960s.

TYPICAL VALUES FOR DIMES

This chart shows prices you'll typically see for the most common dates of each major type of dime, in various conditions. For more detailed pricing, consult the annually issued *Guide Book of United States Coins* (the "Red Book").

Hundreds of millions of silver Mercury dimes were minted during Franklin Roosevelt's three-term presidency. After his death in 1945, Roosevelt would be honored with a new dime bearing his portrait—fitting, given his championing of the "March of Dimes" campaign to end childhood polio.

DIMES	G-4	F-12	EF-40	MS-60	MS-65	PF-63	PF-65
Draped Bust, Small Eagle, 1796–1797	$2,200.00	$4,500	$11,000.00	$26,000.00	$85,000	—	—
Draped Bust, Heraldic Eagle, 1798–1807	500.00	1,000	2,500.00	6,500.00	80,000	$2,750	$7,500
Capped Bust, 1809–1828	35.00	60	450.00	1,400.00	12,000	18,000	40,000
Capped Bust, 1828–1837	30.00	45	300.00	1,000.00	7,500	13,500	30,000
Liberty Seated, No Stars, 1837–1838	45.00	100	500.00	1,100.00	7,750	11,500	30,000
Liberty Seated, With Stars, 1838–1860	16.00	20	50.00	300.00	2,500	1,500	2,500
Liberty Seated, With Arrows, 1853–1855	16.00	20	50.00	300.00	2,500	15,000	25,000
Liberty Seated, With Motto, 1860–1891	15.00	20	35.00	150.00	800	650	1,750
Liberty Seated, With Arrows, 1873–1874	18.00	25	140.00	600.00	4,000	1,500	5,500
Barber, 1892–1916	3.25	4	22.00	110.00	600	600	1,750
Mercury, 1916–1945	2.80	3	3.25	7.00	25	200	375
Roosevelt, silver, 1946–1964	Bullion	Bullion	3.00	3.20	6	4	5

The designs of U.S. dimes, first coined in 1796, follow closely those of half dimes up through the Liberty Seated type, which ended in 1891.

Dimes in each case weigh twice as much as their little sisters.

The earliest dimes—the Draped Bust type dating from 1796 and 1797—are the rarest and most expensive. A very worn 1797 dime (with 13 stars instead of 16), in AG-3 condition, sold for $2,013 in a September 2011 auction. On the other end of the grade scale, an MS-64 dime from 1796 sold for $40,250 in April 2012.

Draped Bust dime, Small Eagle Reverse (1796–1797).

Draped Bust dimes are more readily available, but they still command high prices, and certain varieties are worth even more than the basic dates.

Draped Bust dime, Heraldic Eagle Reverse (1798–1807).

For general grading instructions, see the chapter on "How to Grade Your Coins." You'll find more in-depth instructions for each specific early dime type in *Grading Coins by Photographs*, by Q. David Bowers.

Capped Bust dime (1809–1837).

The Liberty Seated dime had a long run—more than 50 years. It was minted from the mid-1830s, when there were 24 states in the Union and the nation's population was about 13 million, to the early 1890s, with 44 states and nearly 63 million citizens. The coin morphed with minor design changes from time to time (arrows added to the date when the weight was changed; legends moved from reverse to obverse; wreath modified, etc.), but for several generations of Americans the basic motif—Miss Liberty seated, holding a shield and a pole with a Liberty cap—was as familiar as the Roosevelt dime is to us today.

Liberty Seated dime, Variety 1, No Stars on Obverse (1837–1838).

Liberty Seated dime, Variety 2, Stars on Obverse (1838–1853, 1856–1860).

Liberty Seated dime,
Variety 3, Stars on Obverse,
Arrows at Date (1853–1855).

Liberty Seated dime,
Variety 4, Legend on Obverse
(1860–1873, 1875–1891).

Liberty Seated dime,
Variety 5, Legend on Obverse,
Arrows at Date (1873–1874).

GRADING LIBERTY SEATED DIMES

G-4 (Good)—LIBERTY on the shield is worn smooth (unreadable). The date and letters are legible.

VG-8 (Very Good)—The shield is discernible, and at least three letters in LIBERTY are readable.

F-12 (Fine)—LIBERTY is visible, but weak in spots.

VF-20 (Very Fine)—LIBERTY is strong and even.

EF-40 (Extremely Fine)—LIBERTY is strong and the edges of the scroll are distinct.

AU-50 (About Uncirculated)—There is wear on Liberty's shoulder and the high points of her hair.

MS-60 (Uncirculated)—No trace of wear. Light blemishes.

MS-63 (Choice Uncirculated)—Some distracting contact marks or blemishes in prime focal areas. Impaired luster is possible.

PF-63 (Choice Proof)—Nearly perfect.

The following illustrations show what a Good, Very Fine, and Mint State Liberty Seated dime looks like.

G-4
Liberty
Seated
dime
(shown
enlarged).

VF-30
Liberty
Seated
dime (shown
enlarged).

MS-66
Liberty
Seated
dime
(shown
enlarged).

Every Liberty Seated dime is valuable to collectors. Values for common dates are given in the chart at the beginning of this chapter. Some scarcer dates to look for are 1844, 1846, 1856-S, 1858-S, 1859-S, 1860-O, 1863, 1864, 1865, 1866, 1867, 1870-S, 1871-CC, 1872-CC, 1873-CC, 1874-CC, 1879, 1880, 1881, and 1885-S. These scarcer dates are worth hundreds, or even thousands, of dollars even in worn circulated grades.

Proofs were struck in many years, and are valuable.

There is a single known example of the 1873-CC dime. The Carson City Mint struck 12,400 of them, but most of the mintage was melted after the coinage law of 1873 was passed. The only known survivor was auctioned in July 2004 for $891,250, and today is estimated to be worth about $1,500,000!

BARBER DIMES
(1892–1916)

Charles E. Barber, the chief engraver of the U.S. Mint, designed a suite of coinage (the dime, quarter, and half dollar) that debuted in 1892. These coins have long been known by their designer's name. The obverse features a profile of Miss Liberty, modeled after French coinage of the era. The reverse continues the

Barber dime (1892–1916).

"cereal wreath" of various grains, as used on the last round of Liberty Seated dimes. Barber dimes were minted until 1916.

G-4 (Good)—The date and letters are plain. LIBERTY, in the headband, is obliterated.

VG-8 (Very Good)—Some letters in LIBERTY are visible.

F-12 (Fine)—The letters in LIBERTY are visible, but weak in spots.

VF-20 (Very Fine)—LIBERTY is evenly plain.

EF-40 (Extremely Fine)—LIBERTY is sharp and distinct. The edges of the headband are distinct.

AU-50 (About Uncirculated)—There are slight traces of wear on the hair and cheekbone, and on the leaf tips in the wreath.

MS-60 (Uncirculated)—No trace of wear. Light blemishes.

MS-63 (Choice Uncirculated)—Some distracting contact marks or blemishes in prime focal areas. Impaired luster is possible.

PF-63 (Choice Proof)—Nearly perfect.

The following illustrations show what a Good, Very Fine, and Mint State Barber dime looks like.

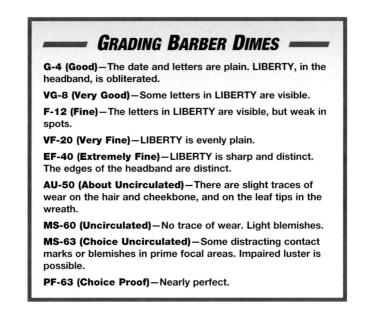

G-4 Barber dime (shown enlarged).

VF-30 Barber dime (shown enlarged).

MS-65 Barber dime (shown enlarged).

Barber dimes are popular among collectors. These were another "workhorse" coin in American commerce, and were still being used in circulation into the early 1950s (although by that time they were definitely vintage, and most had been picked out of pocket change). Most of the dates from the 1890s are more valuable than later dates. Other scarcer dates to look for include the 1900-O, 1901-S, 1903-S, 1904-S, and 1913-S.

There is a variety of 1905-O known as the *Micro O*, with a smaller-than-normal mintmark. It's worth $25 in G-4, $100 to $160 in VF-20, and $350 or more in MS-60.

Proof Barber dimes were struck for collectors every year of the series' run. They're worth between $300 and $1,900 or so, depending on condition. The 1894-S Proof Barber dime is famous (it was ranked among the *100 Greatest U.S. Coins*), with an estimated 24 pieces minted. The reason for this low mintage is unknown; popular theories, among others, include a rounding out of the Mint's record books, or a special presentation to bankers visiting the San Francisco Mint. Today fewer than a dozen examples are known to exist; one sold at auction in October 2007 for $1,552,500.

MERCURY DIMES
(1916–1945)

The Mercury dime is more accurately the *Winged Liberty dime*, because the obverse portrait is not the Roman god Mercury, but Miss Liberty with a winged cap, representing liberty of thought. The reverse shows a fasces, an ancient symbol of authority and unity. These dimes were struck in the tens of millions through both world wars, the Roaring Twenties, and the Great Depression. The design is by sculptor Adolph A. Weinman, who also created the beautiful Walking Liberty half dollar produced in the same era.

Mercury dime (1916–1945).

Mintmark location is on the reverse, left of the fasces.

GRADING MERCURY DIMES

G-4 (Good)—The letters and date are clear. The lines and bands in the fasces are obliterated.

VG-8 (Very Good)—Half of the sticks in the fasces are discernible.

F-12 (Fine)—All the sticks in the fasces are defined. The diagonal bands are worn nearly flat.

VF-20 (Very Fine)—The diagonal bands are definitely visible.

EF-40 (Extremely Fine)—Only slight wear is seen on the diagonal bands. The braids and hair before the ear are clearly visible.

AU-50 (About Uncirculated)—There are slight traces of wear. Most mint luster is present.

MS-60 (Uncirculated)—No trace of wear. Light blemishes.

MS-63 (Choice Uncirculated)—No wear. Attractive mint luster.

PF-63 (Choice Proof)—Nearly perfect.

The following illustrations show what a Good, Very Fine, and Mint State Mercury dime looks like.

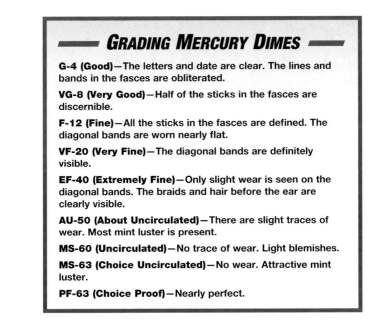

G-4 Mercury dime (shown enlarged).

VF-20 Mercury dime (shown enlarged).

MS-66 Mercury dime (shown enlarged).

Mercury dimes are among the most popular U.S. coin series. They remained in everyday use until the late 1960s, at which time silver was so valuable that many common silver dimes were pulled from circulation and melted. Today all Mercury dimes are valuable—common dates are worth at least $3.00 or so in Fine condition, and $12 in MS-63. Scarcer dates include the 1916-D (worth $1,000 in Good, $4,200 in VF-20, up to $17,000 in MS-63, or even more for higher grades), 1921 ($65 in Good, $320 in VF-20, $1,850 in MS-63), 1921-D ($80 in Good, $420 in VF-20, $1,900 in MS-63), and 1926-S ($13 in Good, $60 in VF-20, $1,500 in MS-63).

ROOSEVELT DIMES
(1946 TO DATE)

President Franklin D. Roosevelt died in 1945 after leading the United States through the Great Depression and most of World War II. To honor his memory, the Treasury rushed to create a new coin: the Roosevelt dime, particularly appropriate given the president's active support of the March of Dimes fundraising efforts to cure polio. The obverse shows his profile portrait, while the reverse features a torch flanked by branches of olive and oak. From 1946 to 1964 the Roosevelt dime was minted in .900 fine silver, after which the rising cost of the precious metal forced Congress to change its composition to copper and nickel. These dimes are common in all dates (with some scarcer die varieties) and are still being minted today. Many can be collected from pocket change to fill a coin folder date by date.

Mercury dime (1916–1945).

The mintmark was on the reverse from 1946 to 1964, and has been on the obverse since 1968.

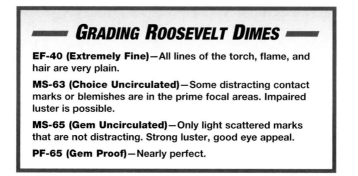

The following illustrations show what a typical Extremely Fine, About Uncirculated, and Mint State Roosevelt dime looks like. (Collectors seldom seek these dimes in grades lower than EF-40.)

EF-40 Roosevelt dime (shown enlarged).

AU-50 Roosevelt dime (shown enlarged).

MS-66 Roosevelt dime (shown enlarged).

Roosevelt dimes of 1946 to 1964 contain .07234 ounce of pure silver, so in any grade they're worth at least their precious-metal content. (See the appendix on bullion values for silver and gold coins.) Copper-nickel dimes of 1965 to date are common, and can be found in circulation. Several collectible die varieties exist (see the *Cherrypickers' Guide to Rare Die Varieties* for examples); one is the 1963 Doubled-Die Reverse, worth $55 in MS-65. In 1982 the P mintmark was omitted from a working die used at the Philadelphia Mint, and the die was used to strike some dimes now known as "No Mintmark." There are two versions of this variety: one with a strong strike, and one with a weak strike. The one with a strong strike is far more valuable and in demand than the weak.

Proofs were minted for collectors from 1950 to 1964, and again from 1968 to date. All are reasonably priced and readily available from coin dealers. Proof die varieties include the 1960 Doubled-Die Obverse and the 1963 Doubled-Die Reverse (each worth $350 in PF-65).

1982, No Mintmark, strong strike. The missing mintmark should be above the date. This variety is worth $225 in MS-65, and $650 in MS-67.

1982, No Mintmark, weak strike. Not as popular as the strong strike, but still valuable, this variety is worth $85 in MS-65, and $300 in MS-67.

14
TWENTY-CENT PIECES

The twenty-cent coin debuted in 1875 as a convenient denomination for making change in the West. (At the time silver coins didn't circulate in the East or Midwest, where they were being hoarded for their silver value.) In the Western states and territories the Spanish "bit" (long valued at 12-1/2 cents) had become the equivalent of a U.S. dime, and nickel five-cent pieces didn't circulate—so when a quarter was offered for a bit purchase, only a dime was handed back in change. The twenty-cent piece, or "double dime," made those transactions smoother.

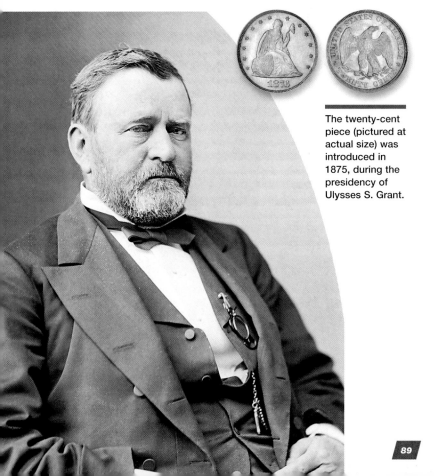

The twenty-cent piece (pictured at actual size) was introduced in 1875, during the presidency of Ulysses S. Grant.

Sometimes people confused the twenty-cent coin for a quarter dollar, because of their similar Liberty Seated designs and their similar size.

The mintage was lowered considerably in 1876 (from more than 1,300,000 to fewer than 25,000 coins), and in 1877 and 1878 the Mint struck only Proof examples.

In spite of their brief production, the coins were still seen in circulation into the early 1900s; by that time, they were often casually used as quarters.

TYPICAL VALUES FOR TWENTY-CENT PIECES

This chart shows prices you'll typically see for the most common twenty-cent piece (the 1875-S), in various conditions. For more detailed pricing, consult the annually issued *Guide Book of United States Coins* (the "Red Book").

TWENTY-CENT PIECES	G-4	F-12	EF-40	MS-60	MS-63	MS-65	PF-63	PF-65
1875–1878	$110	$150	$250	$650	$1,400	$5,500	$3,000	$10,000

— GRADING TWENTY-CENT PIECES —

G-4 (Good)—LIBERTY on the shield is worn smooth (unreadable). The date and letters are legible.

VG-8 (Very Good)—One or two letters in LIBERTY are barely readable. Other details are bold.

F-12 (Fine)—Some letters in LIBERTY are possibly visible.

VF-20 (Very Fine)—LIBERTY is readable, but partly weak.

EF-40 (Extremely Fine)—LIBERTY is mostly sharp. Only slight wear is seen on high points of the coin.

AU-50 (About Uncirculated)—Slight traces of wear are on the breast, head, and knees.

MS-60 (Uncirculated)—No trace of wear. Light blemishes.

MS-63 (Choice Uncirculated)—Some distracting contact marks or blemishes in prime focal areas. Impaired luster is possible.

PF-63 (Choice Proof)—Nearly perfect.

The following illustrations show what a Good, Very Fine, and Mint State twenty-cent piece looks like.

G-4 twenty-cent piece (shown enlarged).

VF-20 twenty-cent piece (shown enlarged).

MS-61 twenty-cent piece (shown enlarged).

The 1875-S is the most common twenty-cent piece, with 1,155,000 minted. All coins in this series are valuable, with the Proofs of 1877 and 1878 worth $2,500 to $3,700 in "impaired" condition (worn down to the equivalent of PF-20 or PF-40), up to $6,000 in PF-63.

15
QUARTER DOLLARS

The 25¢ denomination was authorized by the Act of April 2, 1792, which also established the U.S. Mint and defined the nation's monetary system. The first quarter dollars weren't actually minted until 1796. Since then the quarter has gone through many fascinating design changes, including some wonderful classics, and has become a huge hit among coin collectors and everyday Americans alike. Before 1965 quarters were minted in good old-fashioned U.S. silver, which adds to their appeal today. The State quarter program and other recent issues have made the coin very popular and have introduced millions of Americans to the fun of coin collecting.

George Washington was president when the U.S. Mint was established in Philadelphia in 1792, and when the first quarter dollars were struck in 1796. He would later be honored with his portrait on the coin.

TYPICAL VALUES FOR QUARTER DOLLARS

This chart shows prices you'll typically see for the most common dates of each major type of quarter, in various conditions. For more detailed pricing, consult the latest edition of the *Guide Book of United States Coins* (the "Red Book").

QUARTER DOLLARS	G-4	F-12	EF-40	MS-60	MS-63	MS-65	PF-63	PF-65
Draped Bust, Small Eagle, 1796	$12,000	$26,000	$45,000	$75,000	$125,000	$300,000		
Draped Bust, Heraldic Eagle, 1804–1807	450	950	3,000	9,000	16,000	27,500		
Capped Bust, 1815–1828	100	170	1,350	3,100	6,000	27,000	$40,000	$100,000
Capped Bust, 1831–1838	70	125	400	1,250	4,500	24,000	22,500	65,000
Liberty Seated, No Motto, 1838–1853	23	33	80	450	1,200	5,900	8,500	30,000
Liberty Seated, Arrows and Rays, 1853	22	34	175	900	2,000	15,000	50,000	140,000
Liberty Seated, Arrows, 1854–1855	23	33	75	500	1,100	2,500	17,500	45,000

HALF DIMES	G-4	F-12	EF-40	MS-60	MS-63	MS-65	PF-63	PF-65
Liberty Seated, Motto, 1866–1891	$23	$35.00	$65	$260	$550	$1,800	$950	$2,400
Liberty Seated, Arrows, 1873–1874	23	38.00	225	900	1,650	3,500	1,450	7,000
Barber, 1892–1916	8	22.00	65	225	400	1,100	775	1,900
Standing Liberty, 1916–1917	30	70.00	120	275	350	750		
Standing Liberty, 1917–1930	8	9.00	35	150	225	525		
Washington, silver, 1932–1964	6	6.25	7	8	10	15	9	12

EARLY QUARTERS
(1790s–1830s)

The designs of U.S. quarters follow closely those of the nation's other silver coins up through the Barber type (from the 1790s to the early 1900s).

There was only a negligible coinage of quarters, dimes, and half dimes from the 1790s to 1834. The *Guide Book of United States Coins* estimates that in the year 1830 there was less than one of these silver coins for each person in the country. (That early period was one of chaotic currency made up of bank notes, privately issued paper money, underweight foreign gold coins, foreign silver coins of many types, and fractional U.S. coins.)

Draped Bust quarter,
Small Eagle Reverse (1796).

Draped Bust quarter,
Heraldic Eagle Reverse (1804–1807).

The first quarters didn't have a mark of value, and it wasn't until 1804 that the denomination ("25 C.") was added to the reverse.

Early quarters all are valuable, though not outside the reach of a collector who wants to build a nice collection of circulated coins. The scarcest is the 1796—only 6,146 were minted, and a mere 500 to 600 are estimated to still exist. They're worth $12,000 in Good condition up to $100,000 or more in MS-63 (in August 2010 an MS-65 example sold at auction for $322,000!). Many quarters from the 1800s to late 1830s can be collected for $150 or less in nice Very Good to Very Fine condition.

Capped Bust quarter, Variety 1, Large Diameter (1815–1828).

Capped Bust quarter, Variety 2, Reduced Diameter, Motto Removed (1831–1838).

For general grading instructions, see the chapter on "How to Grade Your Coins." You'll find more in-depth instructions for each specific early quarter type in *Grading Coins by Photographs*, by Q. David Bowers.

LIBERTY SEATED QUARTERS
(1838–1891)

Like the Liberty Seated dime, the quarter dollar of this design clocked more than 50 years as standard U.S. coinage. In the late 1830s, when the first Liberty Seated quarter rolled off the press, there were only about 2,000 miles of completed railroad track in the United States. Sailing ships were the main way of moving commercial goods at sea—a mere 2.5 percent was by steam. By the time the Liberty Seated quarter ended its run in 1891 there was a nationwide network of more than 163,000 miles of railroad, steam shipping was nearly dominant, and the "Great Age of Sail" was over.

Liberty Seated quarter, Variety 1, No Motto Above Eagle (1838–1853, 1856–1865).

Liberty Seated quarter, Variety 2, Arrows at Date, Rays Around Eagle (1853).

Design changes over the years produced several different varieties, all eagerly sought by today's coin collectors.

Liberty Seated quarter, Variety 3, Arrows at Date, No Rays (1854–1855).

Liberty Seated quarter, Variety 4, Motto Above Eagle (1866–1873, 1875–1891).

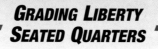

Liberty Seated quarter, Variety 5, Arrows at Date (1873–1874).

GRADING LIBERTY SEATED QUARTERS

G-4 (Good)—The rim is scant. LIBERTY on the shield is worn off. The date and letters are legible.

VG-8 (Very Good)—The rim is fairly well defined. At least three letters in LIBERTY are readable.

F-12 (Fine)—LIBERTY is visible, but weak in spots.

VF-20 (Very Fine)—LIBERTY is strong and even.

EF-40 (Extremely Fine)—LIBERTY is complete and the edges of the scroll are distinct. The clasp of Liberty's gown is clear.

AU-50 (About Uncirculated)—There is slight wear on Liberty's knees and breast and on the eagle's neck, wing tips, and claws.

MS-60 (Uncirculated)—No trace of wear. Light blemishes.

MS-63 (Choice Uncirculated)—Some distracting contact marks or blemishes in prime focal areas. Impaired luster is possible.

PF-63 (Choice Proof)—Nearly perfect.

The following illustrations show what a Good, Very Fine, and Mint State Liberty Seated quarter looks like.

G-4 Liberty Seated quarter (shown enlarged).

VF-20 Liberty Seated quarter (shown enlarged).

MS-66 Liberty Seated quarter (shown enlarged).

All Liberty Seated quarters are valuable to collectors because of their history and relative scarcity. That said, many remain quite affordable in circulated grades. Values for common dates are given in the chart at the beginning of this chapter. Some scarcer dates to look for are 1842-O (the Small Date variety), 1849-O, 1851-O, 1852-O, 1853 (No Arrows or Rays variety), 1854-O (Huge O variety), 1859-S, 1860-S, 1864-S, any date/mint from 1866 to 1870, any date from the Carson City Mint (with a CC mintmark), 1878-S, any Philadelphia Mint coin (with no mintmark) from 1879 to 1890, and 1891-O. These scarcer dates are worth hundreds, or even thousands, of dollars even in worn circulated grades.

Proofs were struck in many years, and are valuable, most ranging from about $1,000 to $2,000 in PF-63.

There are only five known examples of the 1873-CC quarter, which has been ranked among the *100 Greatest U.S. Coins*. The Carson City Mint struck 4,000 of them, but only those few coins are known to have survived. One was auctioned in January 2009 for $431,250!

The suite of coins (dime, quarter, and half dollar) that debuted in 1892 was designed by Charles E. Barber, the chief engraver of the U.S. Mint, and collectors refer to them by their designer's last name. The obverse of the Barber quarter features a profile of Miss Liberty, modeled after French coinage of the era. The reverse has a heraldic eagle. Barber quarters were minted until 1916.

Barber quarter (1892–1916).

GRADING BARBER QUARTERS

G-4 (Good)—The date and letters are legible. LIBERTY, on the headband, is worn off.

VG-8 (Very Good)—Some letters in LIBERTY are visible.

F-12 (Fine)—The letters in LIBERTY are visible, but not sharp.

VF-20 (Very Fine)—LIBERTY is evenly plain.

EF-40 (Extremely Fine)—LIBERTY is bold. The edges of the headband are distinct.

AU-50 (About Uncirculated)—There are slight traces of wear above the forehead, on the cheek, and on the eagle's head, wings, and tail.

MS-60 (Uncirculated)—No trace of wear. Light blemishes.

MS-63 (Choice Uncirculated)—Some distracting contact marks or blemishes in prime focal areas. Impaired luster is possible.

PF-63 (Choice Proof)—Reflective surfaces with only a few blemishes in secondary focal places. No major flaws.

The following illustrations show what a Good, Very Fine, and Mint State Barber quarter looks like.

G-4
Barber
quarter
(shown
enlarged).

VF-30
Barber
quarter
(shown
enlarged).

MS-62
Barber
quarter
(shown
enlarged).

Coin collectors had little interest in saving Barber coinage from circulation until the 1930s. By the time interest was accelerating in the 1940s, Barber quarters were already of a past generation—uncommon sights in pocket change, and set aside when they were noticed by a collector. By that time most were in well-worn grades of AG-3 or Good-4, sometimes VG-8, but rarely nicer. In *Grading Coins by Photographs,* Q. David Bowers notes that "Today, among circulation-strike Barber quarters, probably 90% or more in existence are G-4 or below, a curious situation repeated in the dime and half dollar series." If you find a Barber quarter "in the wild" (in Grandpa's cigar box, or tucked away in a desk drawer) and it's in a higher circulated grade, consider yourself lucky!

Today Barber quarters have a devoted following among coin collectors. Many dates from the 1890s are more valuable than later dates. Look in particular for the 1892-S, 1893-S, 1895-S, 1896-O, 1896-S, 1897-O, 1897-S, 1901-O, 1913-S, and 1914-S.

The 1901-S is a rarity, worth $5,600 in G-4 condition, $22,000 in VF-20, and $37,000 in MS-60. In May 1990 an example graded MS-68 sold at auction for $550,000.

Proofs were struck for every year of the series' run except for 1916. They're generally worth about $800 in PF-63.

STANDING LIBERTY QUARTERS
(1916–1930)

American sculptor Hermon A. Mac-Neil designed the Standing Liberty quarter, which took over from the Barber quarter in 1916. His artistic rendition of Miss Liberty was widely praised from its first appearance. "With her right hand she invites and welcomes the stranger to America," wrote *The Illustrated World* in 1917, "but on the left arm is buckled a shield, and though she offers laurel in token of peace and protection her shield carries forth the idea of strength." The design was timely: in Europe the Great War had been raging for two years, and America would enter the fray before long. The Standing Liberty quarter would go on to be minted through the Roaring Twenties until just after the stock-market crash that presaged the Great Depression. That's a lot of history packed into a brief but significant 15-year series.

Standing Liberty quarter, Variety 1, No Stars Below Eagle (1916–1917).

Standing Liberty quarter, Variety 2, Stars Below Eagle (1917–1930).

Mintmark is located on the obverse, to the left of the date.

The following illustrations show what a Good, Very Fine, and Mint State Standing Liberty quarter looks like.

G-6 Standing Liberty quarter (shown enlarged).

GRADING STANDING LIBERTY QUARTERS

G-4 (Good)—The date and lettering are legible. The top of the date is worn. Liberty's right leg and toes are worn off. Much wear is evident on the left leg and drapery lines.

VG-8 (Very Good)—The date is distinct. The toes are faintly visible. The drapery lines are visible above Liberty's left leg.

F-12 (Fine)—The high curve of the right leg is flat from thigh to ankle. Only slight wear is evident on the left leg. The drapery lines over the right thigh are seen only at the sides of the leg.

VF-20 (Very Fine)—The garment line across the right leg is worn, but visible at the sides.

EF-40 (Extremely Fine)—The design is flattened only at the high spots. Liberty's toes are sharp. The drapery lines across the right leg are evident.

AU-50 (About Uncirculated)—There are slight traces of wear on the head, kneecap, shield's center, and highest point on the eagle's body.

MS-60 (Uncirculated)—No trace of wear, but contact marks, surface spots, or faded luster are possible.

MS-63 (Choice Uncirculated)—No wear. Light blemishes. Attractive mint luster.

VF-20 Standing Liberty quarter (shown enlarged).

MS-64 Standing Liberty quarter (shown enlarged).

Before 1925, the dates on these quarters wore off easily in circulation, because they were too high and weren't protected by other features of the design. In 1925 the Mint redesigned the coin slightly, with a depression in the pedestal on which Liberty stands, bearing the date. The new "recessed" dates proved more durable.

The 1916 Standing Liberty quarter (ranked among the *100 Greatest U.S. Coins*) is the key date of this series; only 52,000 were minted. Today a 1916 is worth $3,250 in Good condition, $10,000 in VF-20, and $15,000 in MS-60. In April 2012 an MS-65 example sold at auction for $29,900.

Uncommon dates include the 1919-D and 1919-S, 1921, 1923-S, 1924-D, and 1927-S.

No Proofs were officially issued.

WASHINGTON QUARTERS
(1932 TO DATE)

New York sculptor John Flanagan designed the Washington quarter, originally intended to be a commemorative coin marking the 200th anniversary of George Washington's birth. Ultimately it was produced as a regular circulation issue. Various modifications have graced the coin over the years, but the profile of President Washington has remained the central obverse motif. The coins were struck in .900 fine silver from 1932 to 1964; since then they've been copper-nickel (with the exception of various silver formats struck for collectors). Proofs for collectors have been made off and on (and, in recent decades, annually) since the early years of the series.

Washington quarter (1932 to date).

Bicentennial quarter (minted in 1975 and 1976, with dual date of 1776–1976).

The following illustrations show what a Good, Very Fine, and Mint State Washington quarter looks like.

G-4 Washington quarter (shown enlarged).

GRADING
WASHINGTON QUARTERS

F-12 (Fine)—The hair lines around Washington's ear are visible. The tiny feathers on the eagle's breast are faintly visible.

VF-20 (Very Fine)—Most hair details are visible. The wing feathers are clear.

EF-40 (Extremely Fine)—The hair lines are sharp. Wear spots are confined to the top of the eagle's legs and the center of the breast.

MS-60 (Uncirculated)—No trace of wear, but many contact marks, surface spotting, or faded luster are possible.

MS-63 (Choice Uncirculated)—No trace of wear. Light blemishes. Attractive mint luster.

MS-65 (Gem Uncirculated)—Only light, scattered marks that are not distracting. Strong luster, good eye appeal.

PF-65 (Gem Proof)—Nearly perfect; hardly any blemishes, and no flaws.

VF-20 Washington quarter (shown enlarged).

MS-64 Washington quarter (shown enlarged).

Washington quarters of 1932 to 1964 contain .18084 ounce of pure silver, so in any grade they're worth at least their precious-metal content. (See the appendix on bullion values for silver and gold coins.) Copper-nickel quarters of 1965 to date are common, and most if not all basic dates can be found in circulation.

In October 1973, the U.S. Treasury announced an open contest for the selection of suitable designs for the reverses of the quarter, half dollar, and dollar, to honor the Bicentennial of the United States. The prize was $5,000 to be awarded to each winner. Twelve semifinalists were chosen, and from these Jack L. Ahr's colonial drummer design was selected for the quarter. Bicentennial quarters were struck in copper-nickel, for circulation, in huge quantities—nearly 1.7 *billion* of them. They're so common that they're not worth more than face value today in circulated grades. If you find a Bicentennial quarter in pocket change, keep it as a good-luck coin, or add it to your collection . . . but if you have a handful it's probably better to spend them than to save them. Higher-grade Mint State examples are worth a few dollars apiece, and the Mint also made collector-quality formats for special sets, including some in silver; those are more valuable, generally worth $4 to $15 apiece.

Many collectible die varieties exist (see the *Cherrypickers' Guide to Rare Die Varieties* for examples); a couple of the copper-nickel varieties are shown here.

1966, Doubled-Die Reverse—
Very strong doubling is visible on all the reverse lettering. This coin is worth $1,000 or more in MS-63, $1,400 in MS-65, and $2,250 in MS-66. In April 2012 an EF-45 example sold at auction for $925.

1966, Doubled-Die Reverse.

1970-D, Doubled-Die Obverse—This extremely rare variety (fewer than a half dozen are known) shows very strong doubling on the date, IN GOD WE TRUST, and the ERTY of LIBERTY. An MS-65 example was auctioned for $2,875 in January 2012.

1970-D, Doubled-Die Obverse.

From 1999 to 2008, the U.S. Mint produced a series of 50 quarter dollars with special reverse designs—five coins per year—honoring the states in the order of their entrance into the Union. These all are legal-tender coins of standard weights and alloys. The obverse, with its portrait of George Washington, was modified to include some of the wording previously used on the reverse.

Each state theme was proposed, and approved, by the governor of that state. Final designs were created by Mint personnel. The quarters were made for circulation at the Philadelphia and Denver mints, and Proofs were made in San Francisco. The State quarter program was very popular, and millions of Americans watched their pocket change, picking out coins they needed for their collections (gathering and displaying them in folders, albums, maps, and other holders). Contests were held for everyday citizens to propose designs, the Mint held special "release" ceremonies as each coin was launched, and people passionately talked about their favorite (and least favorite) designs. All of the excitement encouraged millions of Americans to join the coin-collecting hobby and take a closer look at the coins they used every day. State quarters can still be found in circulation; most are worth only face value, though higher-grade Mint State pieces can be worth a dollar or more.

A selection of various State quarter designs.

At the end of the State quarter program, Congress authorized additional quarters for the District of Columbia and five U.S. territories (Puerto Rico, Guam, American Samoa, the U.S. Virgin Islands, and the Northern Mariana Islands). These were all minted in 2009, and released into circulation just as the State quarters were (in addition to Proofs being made for collectors).

D.C. and Territorial quarters, from 2009.

Following up on the popularity of the 1999–2009 quarter programs, Congress authorized the production of new circulating commemorative quarters from 2010 to 2021. Each coin honors a site of "natural or historic significance" from each of the 50 states, five U.S. territories, and District of Columbia. They continue to bear George Washington's portrait on the obverse. Five designs are being released each year, in the order the coins' featured locations were designated national parks or national sites.

A variety of "America the Beautiful" quarter designs from the Mint's 2010–2021 program.

16
HALF DOLLARS

American commercial interests faced a serious problem in the late 1700s and early 1800s: the government was failing to provide enough coins for circulation. Contrary to popular opinion at the time, this wasn't the Mint's fault; exchange rates and other factors made it profitable for speculators to hinder the free circulation of U.S. gold and silver coins. For example: The U.S. silver dollar was overvalued in relation to the Spanish milled dollar—slightly lighter, and with slightly less pure silver. A speculator could take U.S. dollar coins down to the Caribbean (where they passed at par), exchange them one-for-one with heavier milled dollars, then take the latter to Philadelphia, where the Mint would melt and coin them (free of charge) into U.S. silver dollars, with the excess silver left

David Rittenhouse—surveyor, astronomer, mathematician, and inventor—was the first director of the U.S. Mint. Under his April 1792–June 1795 tenure the nation's first half dollars (and other coins) were produced.

over as profit for the speculator. With such factors in play, most of the new U.S. dollars were exported as fast as they were minted. By 1804 President Thomas Jefferson suspended the coinage of gold eagles ($10 coins) and silver dollars, which led to the *half dollar* being the nation's desirable coin for large transactions and bank reserves. Until 1834, half dollars circulated very little as they were mainly transferred from bank to bank. (This is why a relatively good supply of higher-condition early half dollars is still available to collectors.) In 1830 a Senate committee reported that the nation's silver coinage was considered just so much bullion, and accordingly was "lost to the community" as circulating legal tender.

Legislation of January 18, 1837, revised and standardized the Mint and U.S. coinage laws. The legislation covered legal standards, Mint charges and procedures, legal tender, tolerance in coin weights, accounting methods, a bullion fund, standardization of gold and silver coins to 900 thousandths fineness, and other desirable changes and regulations. With that, U.S. coins (including the half dollar) entered a new modern era.

Since the denomination debuted in 1794, the half dollar has featured many motifs, including one considered by many collectors to be the most beautiful U.S. coin design ever (the Liberty Walking), an homage to early statesman Benjamin Franklin, and a memento to martyred president John F. Kennedy. Hefty and substantial, minted in fine American silver up through the 1960s, the half dollar has an old-time appeal that collectors love. "A collection of half dollars is one of the most satisfying in the American series," notes the *Professional Edition* of the *Guide Book of United States Coins*. "The panorama is extensive. . . . The large size of such pieces makes them convenient to view and enjoy."

TYPICAL VALUES FOR HALF DOLLARS

This chart shows prices you'll typically see for the most common dates of each major type of half dollar, in various conditions. For more detailed pricing, consult the annual *Guide Book of United States Coins* (the "Red Book").

HALF DOLLARS	G-4	F-12	EF-40	MS-60	MS-63	MS-65	PF-63	PF-65
Flowing Hair, 1794–1795	$985	$2,900	$9,500	$42,000	$95,000	$400,000+	—	—
Draped Bust, Small Eagle, 1796–1797	34,000	52,000	100,000	290,000	375,000	$600,000+	$2,750	$7,500
Draped Bust, Heraldic Eagle, 1801–1807	250	350	1,600	8,500	16,250	40,000+	650	1,500
Capped Bust, 1807–1836	60	80	180	1,000	2,000	9,000	40,000	95,000

HALF DOLLARS	G-4	F-12	EF-40	MS-60	MS-63	MS-65	PF-63	PF-65
Capped Bust, 1836–1839	$65	$100	$225	$1,400	$2,900	$16,500	$45,000	$90,000
Liberty Seated, No Motto, 1839–1866	30	50	105	450	1,100	5,250	1,500	5,900
Liberty Seated, Arrows and Rays, 1853	30	55	250	1,450	3,500	8,400	50,000	150,000
Liberty Seated, Arrows, 1854–1855	30	55	125	700	1,700	7,400	12,500	30,000
Liberty Seated, Motto, 1866–1891	30	50	100	475	750	4,000	1,300	3,700
Liberty Seated, Arrows, 1873–1874	35	60	230	950	1,875	17,500	2,650	12,500
Barber, 1892–1915	15	35	190	500	900	2,750	1,200	3,500
Liberty Walking, 1916–1947	14	15	16	35	50	150	400	600
Franklin, 1948–1963	Bullion	Bullion	14	16	18	40	20	22
Kennedy, .900 silver, 1964	Bullion	Bullion	Bullion	15	17	20	15	17
Kennedy, .400 silver, 1965–1970	Bullion	Bullion	Bullion	Bullion	8	15	—	—

EARLY HALF DOLLARS
(1790s–1830s)

Half dollar designs shared the same basic motifs as other silver coins in the 1790s and into the 1830s. Thus we see the Flowing Hair type and various draped and capped busts of Miss Liberty in this era.

The Flowing Hair is readily available in circulated grades and rare in Mint State. Most on the market are dated 1795. In any grade these old coins are valuable—worth between $640 and $2,900 in AG-3 condition, depending on the date; $985 to $4,600 in G-4; $3,900 to $21,000 in VF-20; and $19,000 to $75,000 if you're lucky enough to own one in AU-50. In Mint State, values of $42,000 to $450,000 or more are normal, again depending on the date and the grade.

Flowing Hair half dollar (1794–1795).

Draped Bust half dollar,
Small Eagle Reverse (1796–1797).

Draped Bust half dollar,
Heraldic Eagle Reverse (1801–1807).

Capped Bust half dollar,
Lettered Edge (1807–1836).

Capped Bust half dollar,
Reeded Edge (1836–1839).

The Draped Bust, Small Eagle Reverse, half dollar series is the scarcest among U.S. silver coins made for circulation, worth more than $20,000 even in the most worn-smooth grades. As you move into the 1800s and get into the 1830s, half dollars become easier (more affordable) to collect, as seen in the pricing chart above. Specialists study these coins very carefully, seeking to collect them by minor die varieties.

For general grading instructions, see the chapter on "How to Grade Your Coins." You'll find more in-depth instructions for each specific early half dollar type in *Grading Coins by Photographs*, by Q. David Bowers.

LIBERTY SEATED HALF DOLLARS
(1839–1891)

The U.S. Mint produced half dollars of the Liberty Seated type every year from 1839 to 1891. The designs varied slightly over the years, but always with the basic obverse and reverse motif. Large quantities were minted until 1879, at which time there was a glut of silver coins in American commerce, and after that mintages were reduced.

Liberty Seated half dollar, Variety 1, No Motto
Above Eagle (1839–1853, 1856–1866).

Liberty Seated half dollar, Variety 2,
Arrows at Date, Rays Around Eagle (1853).

Liberty Seated half dollar, Variety 3,
Arrows at Date, No Rays (1854–1855).

Liberty Seated half dollar, Variety 4, Motto Above Eagle (1866–1873, 1875–1891).

Liberty Seated half dollar, Variety 5, Arrows at Date (1873–1874).

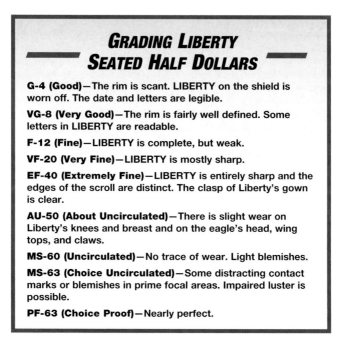

GRADING LIBERTY SEATED HALF DOLLARS

G-4 (Good)—The rim is scant. LIBERTY on the shield is worn off. The date and letters are legible.

VG-8 (Very Good)—The rim is fairly well defined. Some letters in LIBERTY are readable.

F-12 (Fine)—LIBERTY is complete, but weak.

VF-20 (Very Fine)—LIBERTY is mostly sharp.

EF-40 (Extremely Fine)—LIBERTY is entirely sharp and the edges of the scroll are distinct. The clasp of Liberty's gown is clear.

AU-50 (About Uncirculated)—There is slight wear on Liberty's knees and breast and on the eagle's head, wing tops, and claws.

MS-60 (Uncirculated)—No trace of wear. Light blemishes.

MS-63 (Choice Uncirculated)—Some distracting contact marks or blemishes in prime focal areas. Impaired luster is possible.

PF-63 (Choice Proof)—Nearly perfect.

The following illustrations show what a Good, Very Fine, and Mint State Liberty Seated half dollar looks like.

G-6 Liberty Seated half dollar (shown enlarged).

VF-20 Liberty Seated half dollar (shown enlarged).

MS-63 Liberty Seated half dollar (shown enlarged).

Every Liberty Seated half dollar is a valuable piece of American history. Many remain quite affordable in circulated grades, with dozens of dates available for less than $100 in nice VF-20 condition. Values for common dates, by type, are given in the chart at the beginning of this chapter. Some scarcer dates to look for are 1850, 1851, 1852, 1852-O, 1855-S, any date from the Carson City Mint (with a CC mintmark), 1878-S, and every date from 1879 to 1891. These scarcer dates are worth hundreds, or even thousands, of dollars even in worn circulated grades.

Proofs were struck in many years, and are valuable, most ranging from about $1,200 to $1,500 in PF-63.

The 1878-S is a key date in the series. In Good condition it's worth $24,000, and in February 2012 an EF-40 example sold at auction for $86,250.

U.S. Mint chief engraver Charles E. Barber was the designer of the new half dollar that debuted in 1892. Like the dime and quarter of the same type, the Barber half dollar is graced by a strong profile of Miss Liberty wearing a Phrygian cap

Barber half dollar (1892–1915).

and laurels, surrounded by stars. The reverse features a heraldic eagle with outstretched wings, clutching arrows and an olive branch.

The following illustrations show what a Good, Very Fine, and Mint State Barber half dollar looks like.

G-4 Barber half dollar (shown enlarged).

VF-30 Barber half dollar (shown enlarged).

MS-64 Barber half dollar (shown enlarged).

Barber's coins weren't wildly popular in their day—with numismatists or with the general public. Few Barber half dollars were collected while they were being minted (other than Proofs struck for collectors), with the result that most seen today are well worn from circulation, and only a small percentage of surviving coins grade Fine or better. Even the higher-mintage dates are scarce in Mint State. If you find Barber half dollars in a pile of old pocket change, chances are they'll be worn, perhaps almost smooth.

They weren't celebrated as great works of art when they debuted, but today Barber half dollars have a devoted following among coin collectors. All are valuable, even in worn grades, but less-common dates to look for include the 1892-O, 1892-S, 1893-S, 1896-S, 1897-O, 1897-S, 1904-S, 1914, and 1915.

Proofs were struck for every year of the series' mintage. They're generally worth between $1,200 and $1,500 in PF-63.

LIBERTY WALKING HALF DOLLARS
(1916–1947)

A new silver half dollar design debuted in 1916. It was the work of sculptor Adolph A. Weinman, who also created the Mercury dime of that year. Production was intermittent, with none minted in various years of the 1920s and early 1930s, but quantities were generally high, reaching the tens of millions annually in the 1940s.

The coin features a dramatic motif of Miss Liberty striding toward the rising sun, arm outstretched to greet the dawn. On the reverse is an American eagle perched on a rocky crag. This half dollar is widely cited as one of the most attractive designs of all U.S. coinage. In terms of history, a collection of Liberty Walking half dollars makes a formidable display, spanning the Great War, the Roaring Twenties, the Great Depression, and World War II.

Liberty Walking half dollar (1916–1947).

Mintmark location, 1916 and 1917.   Mintmark location, 1917–1947.

GRADING LIBERTY WALKING HALF DOLLARS

G-4 (Good)—The rims are defined. The motto IN GOD WE TRUST is legible.

VG-8 (Very Good)—The motto is distinct. About half of Liberty's skirt lines at the left are clear.

F-12 (Fine)—All skirt lines are evident, but worn in spots. The details of the sandal below the motto are clear.

VF-20 (Very Fine)—Skirt lines are sharp, including in the leg area. There is little wear on the breast and right arm.

EF-40 (Extremely Fine)—All skirt lines are bold.

AU-50 (About Uncirculated)—There is slight trace of wear on Liberty's head, knee, and breasts, and on the eagle's claws and head.

MS-60 (Uncirculated)—No trace of wear. Light blemishes.

MS-63 (Choice Uncirculated)—No wear. Some distracting contact marks or blemishes in prime focal areas. Impaired luster possible.

PF-65 (Gem Proof)—Brilliant surfaces with no noticeable blemishes or flaws. A few scattered, barely noticeable marks or hairlines possible.

The following illustrations show what a Good, Very Fine, and Mint State Liberty Walking half dollar looks like.

G-4
Liberty
Walking
half dollar
(shown
enlarged).

VF-20
Liberty
Walking
half dollar
(shown
enlarged).

MS-65
Liberty
Walking
half dollar
(shown
enlarged).

The value of circulated common-date Liberty Walking half dollars (and most dates are relatively common) is largely based on the current bullion price of silver. Each coin contains .36169 ounce of pure silver, so if the precious metal is trading at $30 per ounce, any Liberty Walking half dollar is worth at least $10.85. Of course, higher grades can be worth considerably more, as these coins are very popular with collectors.

Less-common dates/mintmarks to look for include any from 1916, the 1917-D with obverse mintmark, 1917-S with obverse mintmark, any from 1919, any from 1921, and 1938-D.

Proofs were made from 1936 to 1942, and most are worth about $500 to $1,600, depending on their level of preservation.

FRANKLIN HALF DOLLARS
(1948–1963)

The Franklin half dollar, designed by Mint chief engraver John R. Sinnock, replaced the Liberty Walking motif in 1948. Although the new coin honored one of the greatest Americans of all time, Benjamin Franklin, it generated almost no excitement among coin collectors when it debuted. Still, hobbyists routinely added new dates to their sets to keep them current, and investors saved rolls of the coins.

Franklin half dollar (1948–1963).

The design wasn't missed much when it was replaced in 1964 by the Kennedy half dollar, and by the late 1960s most Franklins had quietly disappeared from circulation; the rising price of silver made them worth more than their face value.

It was up to later generations to fully appreciate the Franklin half dollar. The coin has grown in popularity among collectors—so much so that an award-

Mintmark location, above the Liberty Bell.

winning popular reference, *A Guide Book of Franklin and Kennedy Half Dollars*, was recently published. Today the series is widely and enthusiastically collected.

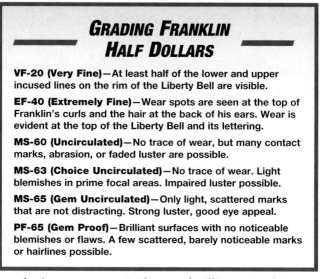

GRADING FRANKLIN HALF DOLLARS

VF-20 (Very Fine)—At least half of the lower and upper incused lines on the rim of the Liberty Bell are visible.

EF-40 (Extremely Fine)—Wear spots are seen at the top of Franklin's curls and the hair at the back of his ears. Wear is evident at the top of the Liberty Bell and its lettering.

MS-60 (Uncirculated)—No trace of wear, but many contact marks, abrasion, or faded luster are possible.

MS-63 (Choice Uncirculated)—No trace of wear. Light blemishes in prime focal areas. Impaired luster possible.

MS-65 (Gem Uncirculated)—Only light, scattered marks that are not distracting. Strong luster, good eye appeal.

PF-65 (Gem Proof)—Brilliant surfaces with no noticeable blemishes or flaws. A few scattered, barely noticeable marks or hairlines possible.

Because they're so common (with tens of millions minted in most years), Franklin half dollars are rarely collected in grades lower than EF-40. Most numismatists seek Mint State and/or Proof examples.

The value of circulated Franklin halves is mainly based on the current bullion price of silver. Each coin contains .36169 ounce of pure silver, so if the precious metal is trading at $35 per ounce, any Franklin half dollar is worth at least $12.66. (See the appendix on bullion values of silver coins.) Of course, higher grades can be worth considerably more, especially if the coin is strongly struck and the bottom lines on the Liberty Bell are completely visible (designated as "Full Bell Lines").

Proofs were made from 1950 to 1963; most are worth about $22 to $85 in PF-65, with pre-1954 Proofs worth substantially more.

KENNEDY HALF DOLLARS
(1964 TO DATE)

Kennedy half dollar (1964 to date).

Mintmark location, 1964.

Mintmark location, 1968 to date.

Bicentennial half dollar (minted in 1975 and 1976, with dual date of 1776–1976).

Gilroy Roberts, chief engraver of the U.S. Mint from 1948 to 1964, designed the obverse of this coin, which features a forceful bust of President John F. Kennedy. The president had been assassinated in November 1963, and Congress quickly sought a fitting commemorative to his life and leadership. The first coinage dies were completed by January 2, 1964. The reverse, by engraver Frank Gasparro, is derived from the presidential coat of arms.

The new coin debuted in .900 fine silver, the same composition as earlier half dollars of that century. The price of silver was rising worldwide, however, and from 1965 to 1970 the alloy was reduced to .400 fine silver. The final mintage of *silver* Kennedy half dollars, in 1970, was reserved for Proof and Mint sets; none were released into circulation.

In October 1973 the U.S. Treasury announced an open contest for new reverse designs for the quarter, half dollar, and dollar, to celebrate the Bicentennial of the United States. The prize was $5,000 to be awarded to each winner. Seth G. Huntington's winning entry, showing Independence Hall in Philadelphia, was featured on the half dollar. More than 500 million Bicentennial halves were struck in copper-nickel for circulation. They're so common that they're not worth more than face value today in circulated grades. If you find a Bicentennial half dollar, keep it as a good-luck coin, or add it to your collection . . . but, as with Bicentennial quarters, it makes more sense to spend them than to save any more than a couple as souvenirs. Higher-grade Mint State examples are worth a few dollars apiece, and the Mint also made collector-quality formats for special sets, including some in silver; those are more valuable, generally worth $5 to $10 apiece.

Kennedy half dollars have been minted every year since their debut, with special formats (including collectible silver strikes) and packaging introduced in recent years. The Philadelphia and Denver mints continue to produce the coins, although only to the tune of a few million each annually, of late. In the years since 2002 these coins have been made available to the public only through direct purchase from the Mint in rolls of 20 or bags of 200 coins. They're not available through banks for general distribution, and are sold by the Mint for approximately 1.5 to 2 times their face value.

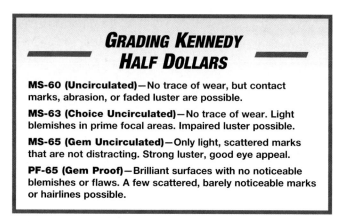

GRADING KENNEDY HALF DOLLARS

MS-60 (Uncirculated)—No trace of wear, but contact marks, abrasion, or faded luster are possible.

MS-63 (Choice Uncirculated)—No trace of wear. Light blemishes in prime focal areas. Impaired luster possible.

MS-65 (Gem Uncirculated)—Only light, scattered marks that are not distracting. Strong luster, good eye appeal.

PF-65 (Gem Proof)—Brilliant surfaces with no noticeable blemishes or flaws. A few scattered, barely noticeable marks or hairlines possible.

Because they're so common (with mintages until recently in the tens or even hundreds of millions of coins every year), Kennedy half dollars are most often collected in Mint State and/or Proof format.

The value of circulated and lower Mint State 1964 coins is based on the current bullion price of silver. Each one contains .36169 ounce of pure silver, so if the precious metal is trading at $32 per ounce, any 1964 half dollar is worth at least $11.57. (See the appendix on bullion values of silver coins.) Of course, higher grades can be worth significantly more, especially if strongly struck; for example, in April 2012 an MS-66 example sold at auction for $127. Millions of 1964 Kennedy half dollars were saved, both in the United States and abroad, and kept in pristine condition as mementoes of the slain president.

The .400 fine silver coins struck for circulation from 1965 to 1969 have .1479 ounce of pure silver. These, too, are valued more for their silver content than for rarity, as hundreds of millions were produced. The 1970-D, made for inclusion in Mint sets, is more of a collector item, with a value of about $18 in MS-63, up to $215 in MS-66.

Proofs have been made of most dates, including silver Proofs in recent collector sets issued by the Mint. Nice examples can be bought for $4 to $30 or so, depending on their level of quality.

17

SILVER AND RELATED DOLLARS

The dollar denomination includes some of the most popular and enthusiastically collected types of all American coinage.

The word *dollar* evolved from the German *thaler*, the name given to the first large-sized European silver coin, which had its start in the Alpine Tyrol in 1484. One of the major producers of these large coins was the mint in the Bohemian city of Joachimsthal ("Valley of St. Joachim"), and so they were popularly called *joachimsthalers*, which was later shortened to *thalers*. The large coins proved so popular in the 1500s that many other countries struck similar pieces, giving them

The U.S. Constitution laid the foundation for the new nation's first silver dollar, granting the national government the authority to "coin Money" and "regulate the Value thereof."

names derived from *thaler*—in the Netherlands, the *rijksdaalder*; in Denmark the *rigsdaler*; in Italy the *tallero*; in Poland the *talar*; in France the *jocandale*.

Eventually the silver deposits in Spain's American colonies would dwarf the production even of Joachimsthal. The Spanish dollar, made with silver from Mexico and central and south America, was widely used and familiar to everyone in the British American colonies. It was only natural, therefore, that the word *dollar* was officially adopted by Congress, on July 6, 1785, for the standard monetary unit of the United States. The silver dollar was congressionally authorized in the Mint Act of April 2, 1792.

Over the centuries since, the dollar coin has gone through many changes in format and design. Today's collectors might be surprised to learn that the silver dollar never circulated to any great extent after 1803, except in the 1840s. The Mint turned out a steady supply of the coins since 1840, but for a variety of reasons (exportation, melting, holding in bank vaults, etc.), the dollar was virtually unseen in American commerce. After the nation effectively went on the gold standard in 1853, the silver dollar was buffeted about by political and economic forces and special interests until the 1930s. Millions of the coins were minted (even when none were needed for business transactions) and then stored away in Treasury vaults. After 1935 the denomination was given a rest, and then it was revived as a copper-nickel coin in 1971. The dollar has since continued to evolve. Today we have smaller golden coins with artistic and historical designs that change every year.

TYPICAL VALUES FOR DOLLAR COINS

This chart shows prices you'll typically see for the most common dates of each major type of dollar, in various conditions. For more detailed pricing, consult the annual *Guide Book of United States Coins* (the "Red Book").

SILVER DOLLARS	G-4	F-12	EF-40	MS-60	MS-63	MS-65	PF-63	PF-65
Flowing Hair, 1794–1795	$1,750	$4,100	$12,000	$65,000	$160,000	$360,000		
Draped Bust, Small Eagle, 1795–1798	1,550	3,000	10,000	55,000	105,000	250,000		
Draped Bust, Heraldic Eagle, 1798–1804	900	1,400	4,600	22,000	56,500	165,000	$500,000	$1,000,000
Gobrecht, 1836–1839			15,500	25,000	45,000	150,000		

SILVER DOLLARS	G-4	F-12	EF-40	MS-60	MS-63	MS-65	PF-63	PF-65
Liberty Seated, No Motto, 1840–1866		$275	$475	$1,900	$5,100	$60,000	$4,500	$15,000
Liberty Seated, Motto, 1866–1873		325	500	2,000	4,350	50,000	3,800	14,000
Trade Dollar, 1873–1883		145	200	950	2,000	11,000	3,100	9,500
Morgan, 1878–1921	Bullion	Bullion	35	45	60	75	2,900	6,100
Peace, 1921–1935	Bullion	Bullion	34	41	50	165	25,000	75,000
Eisenhower, 1971–1978	$1	1	1	1.50	4	10	8	10
Anthony, 1979–1999	1	1	1	1	1	6	5	6
Sacagawea, Native American, and Presidential, 2000 to date	1	1	1	1	1	1.10	4	8

EARLY SILVER DOLLARS
(1790s–1830s)

The Flowing Hair design was used on the earliest U.S. silver dollars, in 1794 and 1795. In the first year only 1,758 were released into circulation; in the next year, nearly 100 times that amount. Many of these coins were used in international trade, especially in the Caribbean. Today, collectors seek out numerous minor variations—the result of early coinage dies being made individually.

Several factors of early Mint technology affected these silver dollars. The silver blanks used to make the coins were weighed before the dollars were struck, and overweight pieces were filed down to remove excess silver. Coins with old adjustment marks from this filing process may be worth less than the values shown in the chart. Some Flowing Hair dollars were weight-adjusted through the insertion of a small (8 mm) silver plug in the center of the blank before the coin was struck.

The Draped Bust design of the late 1700s and early 1800s featured two different reverses, one with a small eagle and the second with a heraldic eagle.

Flowing Hair dollar (1794–1795).

Draped Bust dollar, Small Eagle Reverse (1795–1798).

Draped Bust dollar, Heraldic Eagle Reverse (1798–1804).

Gobrecht dollar (1836–1839).

Congress suspended the minting of silver dollars in 1804, then lifted the suspension in 1831. It wasn't until late in 1835 that dollars (dated 1836) were again struck. The new coins were designed by artist Christian Gobrecht. Only a couple thousand were produced in total—including restrikes made at the Philadelphia Mint from the late 1850s into the 1870s.

All of these early silver dollars are treasured as important artifacts of American history. Collectors value them even in worn-out circulated grades, and in Mint State a single coin can be worth as much as a house . . . with a garage . . . and a new car to go in it.

For general grading instructions, see the chapter on "How to Grade Your Coins." You'll find more in-depth instructions for each specific early dollar type in *Grading Coins by Photographs: An Action Guide for the Collector and Investor.*

An authentic 1804 dollar—one of the rarest and most valuable U.S. coins—of which only 15 are known to exist. These were actually minted in the 1830s. Beware, many modern-day
counterfeits are in the marketplace. If you find an 1804 dollar, remember the adage, "If it looks too good to be true, it probably is." To learn the full story of this fascinating coin, see *The Fantastic 1804 Dollar*, an award-winning classic by Eric P. Newman and Kenneth E. Bressett.

LIBERTY SEATED DOLLARS
(1840–1873)

Starting again in 1840, the U.S. Mint issued quantities of silver dollars for general circulation. The seated figure of Miss Liberty, already in use on some of the nation's smaller silver coins, was adopted for the obverse. The flying eagle design used on the earlier Gobrecht silver dollar was replaced by the more familiar heraldic eagle with a shield, arrows, and olive branch.

Liberty Seated dollar, No Motto (1840–1865).

Liberty Seated dollar, With Motto IN GOD WE TRUST (1866–1873).

By 1850 the silver content of these coins was worth more than their $1 face value. Later issues didn't circulate in the United States but were used mainly in export trade. This situation continued through 1873, when the series was discontinued.

The following illustrations show what a Good, Very Fine, and Mint State Liberty Seated half dollar looks like.

G-4 Liberty Seated dollar (shown enlarged).

VF-20 Liberty Seated dollar (shown enlarged).

MS-65 Liberty Seated dollar (shown enlarged).

Liberty Seated dollars of 1840 to 1850 are available in proportion to their mintages, ranging from a low of 7,500 coins (in 1850) to a high of 184,618 (in 1842). The coins of 1851 to the late 1860s are scarce or rare in circulated grades, and in Mint State they're rare or extremely rare, even though some years had relatively high mintages. The reason is because the later-date coins were shipped to China in commerce, and later were melted. Some coins of the 1870s are more readily available.

Savvy collectors know that many modern-day counterfeit Liberty Seated dollars have been coming out of Asia in recent years. These fakes are made of base metal, and their quality ranges from laughably inept to startlingly deceptive. If you find a Liberty Seated "silver dollar" for sale at a flea market, yard sale, or other non-numismatic venue for what appears to be a bargain price, *think twice* about buying it. Professional third-party certification is recommended, to guarantee authenticity.

TRADE DOLLARS
(1873–1885)

Mintage of standard silver dollars was discontinued in 1873, and a new denomination, the silver *trade dollar*, was authorized by that year's Coinage Act. The new coin, intended to compete with Spanish and Mexican silver dollars in the export trade, was heavier than the old Liberty Seated silver dollar. It was produced in quantity from 1873 to 1885 and was a great success as an international trade coin, especially in China, where merchants preferred silver to gold and refused to accept paper money of any kind.

Trade dollar (1873–1885).

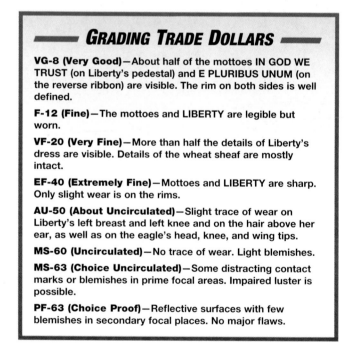

━━━ GRADING TRADE DOLLARS ━━━

VG-8 (Very Good)—About half of the mottoes IN GOD WE TRUST (on Liberty's pedestal) and E PLURIBUS UNUM (on the reverse ribbon) are visible. The rim on both sides is well defined.

F-12 (Fine)—The mottoes and LIBERTY are legible but worn.

VF-20 (Very Fine)—More than half the details of Liberty's dress are visible. Details of the wheat sheaf are mostly intact.

EF-40 (Extremely Fine)—Mottoes and LIBERTY are sharp. Only slight wear is on the rims.

AU-50 (About Uncirculated)—Slight trace of wear on Liberty's left breast and left knee and on the hair above her ear, as well as on the eagle's head, knee, and wing tips.

MS-60 (Uncirculated)—No trace of wear. Light blemishes.

MS-63 (Choice Uncirculated)—Some distracting contact marks or blemishes in prime focal areas. Impaired luster is possible.

PF-63 (Choice Proof)—Reflective surfaces with few blemishes in secondary focal places. No major flaws.

The following illustrations show what a Fine, Extremely Fine, and Mint State trade dollar looks like. (Trade dollars are seldom collected in grades lower than Fine.)

F-12 trade dollar (shown enlarged).

EF-40 trade dollar (shown enlarged).

MS-61 trade dollar (shown enlarged).

The 1878-CC trade dollar is a rarity, but other dates and mintmarks are readily collected in higher-level circulated grades (Extremely Fine and About Uncirculated) and in Mint State. Because the coins didn't circulate for a long time, lower-grade coins (below Fine or so) aren't often seen.

Many trade dollars used in China have counterstamps, called *chopmarks*, which are of interest to collectors. These marks were applied by Chinese bankers and merchants, for accounting purposes or to confirm their silver content. On a Mint State trade dollar a chopmark will decrease its value, but collectors and specialists eagerly seek them on Extremely Fine and About Uncirculated coins.

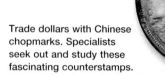

Trade dollars with Chinese chopmarks. Specialists seek out and study these fascinating counterstamps.

Collectors should be aware that many modern-day counterfeit trade dollars lurk in the marketplace. If a coin appears too good to be true, offered at a bargain price, it's probably a fake. *Caveat emptor*—buyer beware!

MORGAN DOLLARS
(1878–1921)

The coinage law of 1873 that authorized the trade dollar for international commerce made no provision for a standard silver dollar to circulate within the United States. For about 15 years the *gold* dollar became the nation's unit coin. Coinage of the silver dollar resumed after legislation of February 28, 1878, known as the Bland-Allison Act. The coin's production benefited Western silver miners by creating an artificial federal demand for the metal, whose value had dropped sharply by 1878. Hundreds of millions of silver dollars were minted, even though they were barely used in day-to-day business, and they piled up in Treasury vaults, stored in cloth bags of 1,000 each.

U.S. Mint engraver George T. Morgan, an award-winning medalist and artist originally from England, designed the new coin. It would be minted every year from 1878 to 1904 (when demand was low and the bullion supply became exhausted), and then again in 1921.

Morgan dollar (1878–1921).

Today Americans love to collect the beautiful and historic Morgan silver dollar. No other coin conjures up so much of the romance and adventure of the United States. Morgan dollars are hefty, they're made of .900 fine U.S. silver, and they have an attractive and distinct design. They're common enough to collect on even a small budget, but the series also has enough rarities and interesting die varieties to engage an advanced collector.

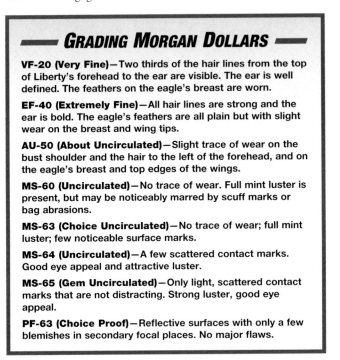

═══ GRADING MORGAN DOLLARS ═══

VF-20 (Very Fine)—Two thirds of the hair lines from the top of Liberty's forehead to the ear are visible. The ear is well defined. The feathers on the eagle's breast are worn.

EF-40 (Extremely Fine)—All hair lines are strong and the ear is bold. The eagle's feathers are all plain but with slight wear on the breast and wing tips.

AU-50 (About Uncirculated)—Slight trace of wear on the bust shoulder and the hair to the left of the forehead, and on the eagle's breast and top edges of the wings.

MS-60 (Uncirculated)—No trace of wear. Full mint luster is present, but may be noticeably marred by scuff marks or bag abrasions.

MS-63 (Choice Uncirculated)—No trace of wear; full mint luster; few noticeable surface marks.

MS-64 (Uncirculated)—A few scattered contact marks. Good eye appeal and attractive luster.

MS-65 (Gem Uncirculated)—Only light, scattered contact marks that are not distracting. Strong luster, good eye appeal.

PF-63 (Choice Proof)—Reflective surfaces with only a few blemishes in secondary focal places. No major flaws.

The following illustrations show what a Good, Very Fine, and Mint State Morgan dollar looks like. Because they're so common and readily available, these coins aren't usually collected in grades lower than VF-20 (except for scarcer varieties).

G-4 Morgan dollar (shown enlarged).

VF-20 Morgan dollar (shown enlarged).

MS-61 Morgan dollar (shown enlarged).

In the 1960s and 1970s the Treasury opened its vaults and released hoards of its stored-away Morgan dollars. These included many date/mintmark combinations, including some that were considered scarce before the Treasury release, and also millions of Carson City coins, which are increasingly popular in today's market. Collectors and investors were excited by the government's sales of these huge quantities of Morgan dollars, and bought them up with gusto, with the result that today they are the most widely collected of all coins of the era.

A Morgan dollar contains .77344 ounce of pure silver, so even in the most worn-out grade it has some value. (For example, if silver is trading at $34 per ounce a Morgan dollar has about $26 worth of the precious metal, not even counting its numismatic value. See the appendix on bullion values for more information.)

In addition to regular dates and mintmarks, serious collectors are passionate about the many die varieties in the Morgan dollar series. The following are just a few of the more popular varieties. Others are pictured in the *Guide Book of United States Coins, Professional Edition*, and the *Cherrypickers' Guide to Rare Die Varieties*.

1888-O, Obverse Die Break—Nicknamed the "Scarface" variety, this Morgan dollar has a dramatic break running across Liberty's face and neck. An MS-62 example sold at auction in April 2012 for $12,650 (compare that to the value of a normal 1888-O, about $60).

1890-CC, Die Gouge—On the reverse of the "Tailbar" variety, a heavy die gouge extends from between the eagle's first tail feather and the lowest arrow feather to the leaves in the wreath below. "This is an extremely popular and highly marketable variety," says the *Cherrypickers' Guide*, "especially in Mint State." In April 2012 an AU-55 example sold at auction for $700.

1888-O, "Scarface" variety.

1890-CC, "Tailbar" variety.

The following chart gives the values of every basic date/mintmark of these popular coins.

MORGAN DOLLARS	VF-20	EF-40	AU-50	MS-60	MS-65	PF-63
1878, 8 Feathers	$45	$50	$70	$135	$1,600	—
1878, 8 Feathers, Proof	—	—	—	—	—	$3,500
1878, 7 Over 8, Clear Doubled Feathers	35	50	73	140	2,450	—
1878, 7 Feathers, 2nd Reverse	33	40	45	68	1,200	—
1878, 7 Feathers, 2nd Reverse, Proof	—	—	—	—	—	3,450
1878, 7 Feathers, 3rd Reverse	35	40	50	88	2,500	—
1878, 7 Feathers, 3rd Reverse, Proof	—	—	—	—	—	60,000
1878CC	100	140	150	260	1,750	—
1878S	35	40	45	60	285	—
1879	34	36	40	50	850	—
1879, Proof	—	—	—	—	—	3,000
1879CC, CC Over CC	290	770	1,750	3,800	44,500	—

MORGAN DOLLARS	VF-20	EF-40	AU-50	MS-60	MS-65	PF-63
1879CC, Clear CC	$290	$750	$1,850	$4,200	$30,000	—
1879O	35	40	47	85	3,500	—
1879S, 2nd Reverse	40	45	58	135	6,500	—
1879S, 3rd Reverse	34	37	41	50	175	—
1880	34	37	41	53	725	—
1880, 80 Over 79	36	38	55	100	3,300	—
1880, Proof	—	—	—	—	—	$2,850
1880CC, 80 Over 79, 2nd Reverse	220	285	350	600	3,000	—
1880CC, 8 Over 7, 2nd Reverse	210	285	325	550	2,700	—
1880CC, 8 Over High 7, 3rd Reverse	210	275	325	500	1,300	—
1880CC, 8 Over Low 7, 3rd Reverse	270	365	475	600	1,400	—
1880CC, 3rd Reverse	210	275	325	460	1,250	—
1880O	34	36	43	75	27,500	—
1880S	34	37	41	50	175	—
1881	34	37	42	53	690	—
1881, Proof	—	—	—	—	—	2,850
1881CC	425	450	475	525	900	—
1881O	34	37	41	50	1,500	—
1881S	34	37	41	50	175	—
1882	34	37	41	50	500	—
1882, Proof	—	—	—	—	—	2,850
1882CC	120	130	145	185	460	—
1882O	34	37	42	50	1,200	—
1882S	34	37	41	50	175	—
1883	34	37	41	50	200	—
1883, Proof	—	—	—	—	—	2,850
1883CC	120	130	145	185	475	—
1883O	34	37	41	50	175	—
1883S	36	53	180	650	42,000	—

MORGAN DOLLARS	VF-20	EF-40	AU-50	MS-60	MS-65	PF-63
1884	$34	$37	$41	$50	$340	—
1884, Proof	—	—	—	—	—	$2,850
1884CC	120	130	145	185	475	—
1884O	34	37	41	50	175	—
1884S	40	60	290	7,200	250,000	—
1885	34	37	41	50	175	—
1885, Proof	—	—	—	—	—	2,850
1885CC	475	500	525	550	1,100	—
1885O	34	37	41	50	175	—
1885S	50	63	130	235	2,000	—
1886	34	37	41	50	175	—
1886, Proof	—	—	—	—	—	2,850
1886O	37	45	95	750	185,000	—
1886S	78	93	160	310	3,000	—
1887	34	37	41	50	175	—
1887, Proof	—	—	—	—	—	2,850
1887O	37	42	55	70	2,350	—
1887S	40	48	60	135	2,600	—
1888	34	37	41	50	215	—
1888, Proof	—	—	—	—	—	2,850
1888O	34	37	41	50	575	—
1888S	165	185	205	290	3,200	—
1889	34	37	41	50	365	—
1889, Proof	—	—	—	—	—	2,850
1889CC	1,400	2,750	6,000	24,000	325,000	—
1889O	34	37	55	165	7,200	—
1889S	60	75	105	210	2,200	—
1890	34	37	43	53	2,650	—
1890, Proof	—	—	—	—	—	2,850
1890CC	110	165	200	440	5,000	—
1890O	34	37	49	75	2,200	—
1890S	34	37	45	70	1,150	—

MORGAN DOLLARS	VF-20	EF-40	AU-50	MS-60	MS-65	PF-63
1891	$35	$38	$45	$65	$8,500	—
1891, Proof	—	—	—	—	—	$2,850
1891CC	110	155	210	375	4,750	—
1891O	37	40	55	165	8,200	—
1891S	35	40	45	70	1,500	—
1892	43	53	90	185	4,750	—
1892, Proof	—	—	—	—	—	2,850
1892CC	285	450	690	1,400	8,250	—
1892O	40	48	70	190	7,500	—
1892S	140	325	1,650	36,000	190,000	—
1893	195	250	350	725	7,500	—
1893, Proof	—	—	—	—	—	2,850
1893CC	625	1,400	2,100	3,800	70,000	—
1893O	325	525	800	2,400	220,000	—
1893S	5,000	8,250	20,000	97,500	650,000	—
1894	1,250	1,500	1,750	3,500	44,000	—
1894O	60	115	260	675	65,000	—
1894S	95	165	400	675	6,000	—
1895, Proof	33,500	35,000	38,000	45,000	77,500	49,000
1895O	400	600	1,350	14,500	170,000	—
1895S	900	1,200	1,800	3,900	27,500	—
1896	34	37	41	50	240	—
1896, Proof	—	—	—	—	—	2,850
1896O	37	43	160	1,400	175,000	—
1896S	70	240	775	1,800	18,000	—
1897	34	37	41	50	325	—
1897, Proof	—	—	—	—	—	2,850
1897O	34	41	115	700	65,000	—
1897S	34	37	45	68	600	—
1898	34	37	41	50	250	—
1898, Proof	—	—	—	—	—	2,850

MORGAN DOLLARS	VF-20	EF-40	AU-50	MS-60	MS-65	PF-63
18980	$34	$37	$41	$50	$195	—
1898S	40	50	100	275	2,450	—
1899	180	200	225	265	950	—
1899, Proof	—	—	—	—	—	$2,850
18990	34	37	40	50	195	—
1899S	48	65	120	340	2,000	—
1900	34	37	41	50	195	—
1900, Proof	—	—	—	—	—	2,850
19000	34	37	41	50	205	—
1900S	35	48	100	300	1,650	—
1901	50	115	350	2,300	375,000	—
1901, Proof	—	—	—	—	—	2,850
19010	34	37	41	50	190	—
1901S	45	65	210	475	3,250	—
1902	34	37	45	55	485	—
1902, Proof	—	—	—	—	—	2,850
19020	34	37	45	55	200	—
1902S	120	175	250	365	2,800	—
1903	50	55	65	78	325	—
1903, Proof	—	—	—	—	—	2,850
19030	310	340	365	400	650	—
1903S	205	350	1,600	3,900	11,500	—
1904	40	47	55	95	3,000	—
1904, Proof	—	—	—	—	—	2,850
19040	34	37	41	50	185	—
1904S	90	215	550	1,350	10,500	—
1921	33	35	36	45	190	—
1921, Proof	—	—	—	—	—	—
1921D	33	35	36	48	400	—
1921S	33	35	36	48	1,500	—

PEACE DOLLARS
(1921–1935)

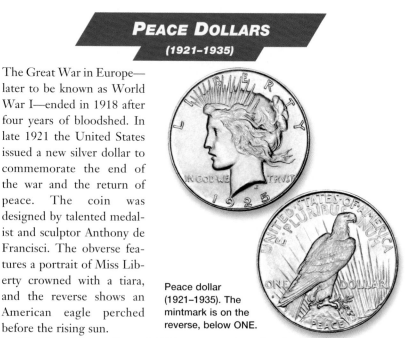

The Great War in Europe—later to be known as World War I—ended in 1918 after four years of bloodshed. In late 1921 the United States issued a new silver dollar to commemorate the end of the war and the return of peace. The coin was designed by talented medalist and sculptor Anthony de Francisci. The obverse features a portrait of Miss Liberty crowned with a tiara, and the reverse shows an American eagle perched before the rising sun.

Peace dollar (1921–1935). The mintmark is on the reverse, below ONE.

The first Peace dollars of 1921 were struck with a high relief; this caused weakness in the centers, so the design was changed to low relief in 1922. The coins were produced every year until 1928, then again in 1934 and 1935. "After languishing for much of the previous dozen years, demand for coins seemed to jump [in the early 1930s], pushing the mints to work hard to keep up the pace," writes Roger W. Burdette in the *Guide Book of Peace Dollars*. "In part, commercial demand was increasing, but the government also was producing more coins because it was profitable to do so. By forcing large quantities of new coin through the Federal Reserve System to commercial banks, the appearance of greater prosperity was carried to the man on the street. The reasons for striking silver dollars in 1934 and 1935—coins that had no commercial use and were not wanted by merchants—are embedded in the Roosevelt Administration's attempts to pull the nation out of depression and the political involvement in Western states' silver-mining interests." Coinage stopped after 1935, and during World War II the government melted many of its stored silver dollars to have their metal for various wartime uses.

Legislation in 1964 authorized the coinage of 45 million silver dollars, and 316,076 new Peace dollars dated 1964 were struck at the Denver Mint in 1965. Plans for completing the coinage were abandoned before any of the coins were released, and the entire mintage was melted. None were preserved or released into circulation. Today the 1964 Peace dollar is a famous "What might have been?" coin, and some theorists enjoy pondering if there was any way for an example or two to have escaped the melting. The full story of the 1964-D Peace dollar is told in Burdette's *Guide Book of Peace Dollars*.

GRADING PEACE DOLLARS

VF-20 (Very Fine)—The hair over Liberty's eye is well worn. Some strands over the ear are well defined. Some eagle feathers on the top and outside edge of the right wing are visible.

EF-40 (Extremely Fine)—The hair lines over the brow and ear are strong, though slightly worn. The outside wing feathers at the right and those at the top are visible but faint.

AU-50 (About Uncirculated)—Slight traces of wear. Most of the mint luster is present, although marred by contact marks.

MS-60 (Uncirculated)—No trace of wear. Full mint luster, but possibly noticeably marred by stains, surface marks, or bag abrasions.

MS-63 (Choice Uncirculated)—No wear. Some distracting contact marks or blemishes in prime focal areas. Impaired luster possible.

MS-64 (Uncirculated)—A few scattered contact marks. Good eye appeal and attractive luster.

MS-65 (Gem Uncirculated)—Only light, scattered contact marks that are not distracting. Strong luster, good eye appeal.

The following illustrations show what a Fine, Extremely Fine, and Mint State Peace dollar looks like.

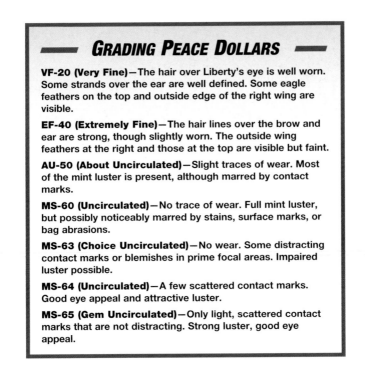

F-12 Peace dollar (shown enlarged).

EF-40 Peace dollar (shown enlarged).

MS-64 Peace dollar (shown enlarged).

The value of common-date (which includes most of them) Peace dollars in circulated grades lies in the .900 fine silver they're made of. With .77344 ounce of pure silver, any given Peace dollar is worth, for example, $23.20 when silver is trading at $30 an ounce, or $27.07 when it's at $35 an ounce. (See the appendix on bullion values of common silver coins.) Of course, that's only their precious-metal value; higher grades, scarcer dates, and rare die varieties command stronger prices.

The 1921 High Relief, 1928, and 1934-S are three less-common dates to look for. Some Peace dollars are inexpensive in lower grades, but much more valuable (compared to others similarly priced in circulated condition) in higher grades. The 1924-S, 1925-S, 1927-D and 1927-S, 1928 and 1928-S, and 1935-S fall into that category.

EISENHOWER DOLLARS
(1971–1978)

Eisenhower dollar (1971–1978).

Bicentennial dollar (minted in 1975 and 1976, with dual date of 1776–1976).

A new dollar coin was introduced in 1971, more than 30 years after the last Peace dollars rolled out of the Mint. The coin, the same size as its predecessor, honored president and World War II hero Dwight D. Eisenhower (who had passed away in 1969) and also the first landing of man on the moon (also in 1969). Chief Engraver Frank Gasparro designed the coin with a profile of Eisenhower and an adaptation of the official Apollo 11 insignia (an American eagle landing with an olive branch on the moon).

A special reverse design was issued for the nation's bicentennial in 1976. Nearly a thousand entries had been submitted after the Treasury announced an open competition to design the coin in October 1973. The winner was Dennis R. Williams's rendition of the Liberty Bell superimposed over the moon. The obverse remained unchanged except for the dual date 1776–1976. Bicentennial dollars were included in various offerings of Proof and Uncirculated coins made by the Mint. More than 220 million were also issued for general circulation. A good number of the coins made their way into American casinos, where they were used as gambling stakes.

Although some "Ike" dollars (as they're sometimes called) were struck in .400 fine silver and sold by the Mint in collectible formats, most of them were made in an alloy of copper and nickel, for circulation. Old habits die hard, so even today many people popularly refer to them as "silver dollars," because they're the same size as the older Peace and Morgan dollars, which were indeed coined of .900 fine silver.

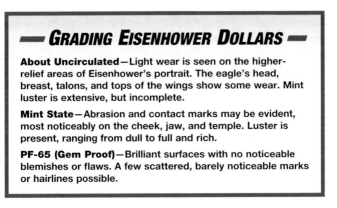

GRADING EISENHOWER DOLLARS

About Uncirculated—Light wear is seen on the higher-relief areas of Eisenhower's portrait. The eagle's head, breast, talons, and tops of the wings show some wear. Mint luster is extensive, but incomplete.

Mint State—Abrasion and contact marks may be evident, most noticeably on the cheek, jaw, and temple. Luster is present, ranging from dull to full and rich.

PF-65 (Gem Proof)—Brilliant surfaces with no noticeable blemishes or flaws. A few scattered, barely noticeable marks or hairlines possible.

Collectors rarely seek Eisenhower dollars in grades lower than AU-50, because they're so common. Nice Mint State and Proof examples are readily available.

You can still sometimes get Eisenhower dollars from your local bank, for face value, and store cashiers will occasionally receive an Ike or two in the course of everyday business. Former American Numismatic Association governor and longtime collector Bill Fivaz likes to give them as restaurant tips, knowing they'll spark conversation and possibly interest others in coin collecting.

In higher Mint State grades (MS-65 and 66 or finer), Ikes can be worth $20 to $30 or more, up to several hundred dollars. In April 2012 an MS-66 example of the 1973 dollar sold at auction for $1,093.

Congress on October 10, 1978, authorized a new coin that would honor a pioneer in women's rights. U.S. Mint chief engraver Frank Gasparro designed the profile portrait of Susan B. Anthony on the obverse, and the reverse picked up his motif of an eagle

Susan B. Anthony dollar (1979–1999).

landing on the moon, from the 1971–1978 Eisenhower dollar. This dollar marked the first time a woman (other than a model or a symbolic figure) appeared on a circulating U.S. coin.

The Anthony dollar was the United States' first small-sized dollar coin, thinner than earlier types, and measuring 26.5 mm compared to 38.1 mm. The Treasury hoped that they would be a cost-efficient substitute for *paper* dollars (costing more to produce per unit, but lasting considerably longer in circulation—about 20 years, compared to less than 2 years for a paper $1 note). Numismatic historian Q. David Bowers, in the *Expert's Guide to Collecting and Investing in Rare Coins*, explains why the Anthony dollar wasn't a success. "First of all, the coin was too small," he writes, "nearly the size of a quarter dollar, and could easily be mistaken for it. . . . [A]fter the first pieces were minted, Gasparro spent one in the cafeteria at the Mint, where it was immediately accepted as a quarter without question. Second, generally in American financial history one type of instrument is preferred for a given denomination in general commerce. As paper dollars were still being made in quantity, the Anthony dollar did not fill a need. Had paper dollars been eliminated, the convenience of the new coins might have been much greater. Third, vending machines . . . were not fitted to take the Anthony dollars. These unfortunate factors came together with the result that the public spurned them."

A large mintage in 1979 was followed by smaller quantities in 1980 and 1981, and then a hiatus of almost 20 years. A final mintage of more than 41 million coins was produced in 1999, perhaps to meet the needs of the vending-machine industry.

Because these coins are so common as a type (minted in the hundreds of millions), and because well-struck Mint State and Proof examples are so readily available, collectors rarely seek them in grades less than About Uncirculated.

Anthony dollars are still dispensed by some vending machines as change. Higher-grade Mint State examples are worth a premium (for example, in July 2009 a 1979-D graded MS-67 was sold at auction for $299), but in general they can be collected for face value. A notable variety is the 1979-P "Wide Rim." In 1979 the obverse design was modified to widen the border rim; those coins struck late in the year with the wider rim are worth about $38 in MS-64, $55 in MS-65, or $135 in MS-66.

GRADING SUSAN B. ANTHONY DOLLARS

About Uncirculated—Light wear is seen on the higher-relief areas of Anthony's portrait. The eagle's head, breast, talons, and tops of the wings show some wear. Mint luster is extensive, but incomplete.

Mint State—Abrasion and contact marks may be evident, most noticeably on the cheek and upper center of the hair. Luster is present, ranging from dull to full and rich.

PF-65 (Gem Proof)—Brilliant surfaces with no noticeable blemishes or flaws. A few scattered, barely noticeable marks or hairlines possible.

1979-P, Narrow Rim (the "Far Date" variety).

1979-P, Wide Rim (the less common, more valuable "Near Date" variety).

MODERN-DAY "GOLDEN" DOLLARS
(2000 TO DATE)

Since 2000 the U.S. Mint has produced several programs, some of which are ongoing, of small-sized dollars made of pure copper with an outer layer of manganese brass. The coins are called "golden dollars" because of their bright gold color in Mint State. The new cop-

Sacagawea dollar (2000–2008).

per / manganese-brass composition and the coins' smooth edge were mandated under the U.S. Dollar Coin Act of 1997. The distinctive golden color and the lack of reeding on the edge help distinguish these dollars from similarly sized quarter dollars.

Even though some vending machines dispense them as change, golden dollars haven't circulated actively. Like Morgan silver dollars in the early 1900s, today's dollar coins—hundreds of millions of them—are sitting in bags in Treasury vaults. Since 2011 the Mint has been producing them only for numismatic sales (as opposed to distributing them for circulation).

The first of these new coins, the Sacagawea dollar (2000–2008), was selected from 120 submissions in a national competition. The winning motif was by artist Glenna Goodacre. It features Sacagawea, a young Native American Shoshone who served as an interpreter and guide to explorers Meriwether Lewis and William Clark during their famous early-1800s journey westward from the great northern plains to the Pacific Ocean. On her back Sacagawea carries her infant son, Jean Baptiste.

For 2002, 2007, and 2008, the Mint produced millions of Sacagawea dollars in Philadelphia and Denver but didn't issue the coins for circulation through banks, instead making them available to the general public through direct sales.

The Sacagawea dollar was modified into the Native American dollar in 2009. Since that year the reverse of the golden dollar has featured an annually changing design that memorializes Native Americans and, in the words of the authorizing legislation, "the important contributions made by Indian tribes and individual Native Americans to the development [and history] of the United States." The Native American $1 Coin Act also called for edge marking on the coins. The year of minting and mintmark are incused on the edge, as is the inscription E PLURIBUS UNUM.

Native American dollars (2009 to date).

Former presidents of the United States are honored on another series of golden dollars. Presidential dollars were issued for circulation from 2007 through 2011, and since 2012 have been offered by the Mint for numismatic sales only, in various collectible sets and special finishes. Four different coins are issued each year, in the order that the presidents served. The reverse of each coin has a design featuring the Statue of Liberty. Originally the date, the mintmark, and the motto IN GOD WE TRUST were on the coins' edge; the motto was moved to the obverse starting in 2009.

Golden dollars are plentiful enough that circulated examples can be collected for face value. To order 40-coin rolls, 100-coin bags, or 250-coin boxes of the latest Presidential and Native American dollars, or to collect the Mint's special strikings (including Proofs), you can visit www.USMint.gov.

A selection of Presidential dollars (2007–2016).

The edges of the Presidential
dollars have been used for the
date, mintmark, and legends.

18
GOLD COINS

Gold has served as money or established the monetary value of currencies longer than any other material. The use of gold coins was widespread in Europe by 300 B.C. In the region that became the United States of America, the earliest circulating coins were foreign, mostly silver and gold—some brought from Europe, some made in Spanish territories in the New World. After Britain's colonies declared and won their independence, a 1792 congressional act established the new nation's independent monetary system, with the dollar as the basic U.S. monetary unit containing 24-3/4 grains of fine gold, based on the world price of $19.39 per troy ounce (480 grains).

In a famous 1900 reelection poster, President William McKinley is supported by American business-men and workers, standing atop "Sound Money" as symbolized by a giant gold coin.

The United States minted gold coins for circulation from the mid-1790s to the early 1930s, in denominations ranging from $1 to $20.

The first U.S. gold coins were half eagles ($5 coins) struck in the summer of 1795. These were soon followed by eagles ($10) and, in 1796, quarter eagles ($2.50). With the price of gold varying between the United States and European markets, it was profitable for speculators to export U.S. gold coins abroad, where they were more valuable—as a result, the coins were almost never seen in circulation in the States. In 1804 the federal government, realizing that it was shoveling gold into a faraway furnace, halted coinage of $10 gold coins. This didn't stop the drain, as the Mint's smaller-denomination coins also continued to be exported. On June 28, 1834, Congress reduced the authorized weight of the nation's gold coins so that their bullion value was slightly less than their face value. This fixed the problem by making U.S. gold coins less tempting to foreign markets, removing the incentive to export them en masse, and thus keeping them at home. U.S. gold coins once again circulated far and wide in the United States. (There would be exceptions to that robust circulation—for example in the Civil War / Reconstruction era from 1861 to 1879. In those years gold coins were hoarded in the Eastern and Midwest states, although they continued to be exchanged on the West Coast.)

The California Gold Rush that started in 1848 brought a flood of the precious metal, along with two new federal coins. The first gold dollars were minted for circulation in 1849, and the first $20 coins (double eagles) in 1850. The double eagle was a success, being very convenient for large transactions domestically, and also a popular coin for international trade. Eventually more than three-quarters of all precious metal converted into coins in the United States would be in the form of double eagles.

In 1854 a new denomination was born: the $3 gold piece. It never was popular with the public, even though one of the coins might conveniently buy 100 postage stamps, or could be exchanged for 100 silver trimes, which were also in circulation. Still, the Mint kept up its production until 1889, after which both the $3 and the $1 gold coins were retired. Meanwhile the Mint's presses were kept busy coining quarter eagles, half eagles, eagles, and double eagles.

In 1933 President Franklin Roosevelt signed Executive Order 6102, forbidding the hoarding of gold. The president's order was designed to protect the nation's banking system, which was fragile in the early years of the Great Depression. It required "all persons" to "deliver on or before May 1, 1933 all gold coin, gold bullion, and Gold Certificates now owned by them to a Federal Reserve Bank, branch or agency, or to any member bank of the Federal Reserve System." Criminal penalties for violation of the order were a fine of up to $10,000 or jail time of up to 10 years—or both. (Exceptions were made for reasonable amounts of gold used in industry, professions like dentistry, and the arts; rare coins owned by collectors; and a few other special cases. Also, individuals could hold small amounts of gold coinage—up to $100 but no more.) The dollar price of gold was set at $35 per ounce in 1934. Use of gold in international trade was further restricted as the price rose. The government revalued gold at $38 per ounce in

1972, then $42.22 in 1973. In 1974 Congress and President Gerald Ford re-legalized the private ownership of gold coins, bars, and certificates, effective December 31. After more than 40 years, Americans could once again legally own as much gold as they wanted. Since then the value of gold on the open market has fluctuated, in particular with dramatic increases in recent years.

Today U.S. gold coins are hot collectibles. They're small but beautiful works of art (some designed by famous artists like Augustus Saint-Gaudens and Bela Lyon Pratt); and at the same time, they're internationally recognized standards of bullion value, easily stored and transported, legal tender, and with precious-metal fineness guaranteed by the U.S. government. In other words, they have everything to appeal to both serious numismatists and investment-minded speculators.

Early gold coins (1790s and early 1800s) are far more valuable as numismatic collectibles than as mere bullion. Collectors pay thousands of dollars even for circulated examples in Fine or Very Fine condition. Similarly, gold $1 and $3 coins are valued more as rare coins than as precious metal. On the other hand, the more common coins of the $2.50, $5, $10, and $20 denominations are valued based on their bullion, plus a small numismatic premium. Of course, each gold coin type has its scarce and rare dates.

The gold U.S. coins most commonly found in Grandpa's cigar box or tucked away in small collections are of the Liberty Head type. This design was used on quarter eagles from 1840 to 1907; on half eagles from 1839 to 1908; on eagles from 1866 to 1907; and on double eagles from 1849 to 1907.

Other gold coins frequently seen include Indian Head quarter eagles and half eagles of 1908 to 1929; Indian Head eagles of 1907 to 1933; and Saint-Gaudens double eagles of 1907 to 1932.

Liberty Head $1
(1849–1854).

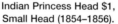

Indian Princess Head $1,
Small Head (1854–1856).

Indian Princess Head $1,
Large Head (1856–1889).

Capped Bust to Right $2.50
(1796–1807).

Capped Bust to Left $2.50 (1808).

Capped Head to Left $2.50
(1821–1834).

Classic Head $2.50 (1834–1839). Scarcer dates include 1838-C, 1839-C, and 1839-D.

Liberty Head $2.50 (1840–1907). Scarcer
dates include 1841, 1854-D, 1854-S, 1855-D,
1856-D, 1859-D, 1864, 1865, 1875, and 1881.

Indian Head $2.50
(1908–1929). The
scarcest date is 1911-D.

Indian Princess Head $3
(1854–1889). Scarcer dates
include 1854-D, 1854-O,
1865, 1873, 1877, and 1881.

Capped Bust to Right $5,
Small Eagle Reverse (1795–1798).

Capped Bust to Right $5,
Heraldic Eagle Reverse (1795–1807).

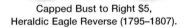

Capped Bust to Left $5 (1807–1812).

Capped Head to Left $5 (1813–1834).

Classic Head $5 (1834–1838). Scarcer
dates include 1834 (Crosslet 4
variety), 1838-C and 1838-D.

Liberty Head $5 (1839–1908). Scarcer
dates include 1842-C (Small Date),
1861-C, 1861-D, 1864-S, 1870-CC,
1873-CC, 1875, and 1878-CC.

Indian Head $5
(1908–1929).
Scarcer dates
include 1909-O
and 1929.

Capped Bust to Right $10, Small Eagle (1795–1797).

Capped Bust to Right $10, Heraldic Eagle (1797–1804).

Liberty Head $10 (1838–1907). Scarcer dates include 1838, 1841-O, 1855-S, 1859-O, 1859-S, 1860-S, 1863, 1864-S, 1865-S, 1866-S, 1867-S, 1870-CC, 1871-CC, 1872-CC, 1873, 1873-CC, 1875, 1875-CC, 1876, 1876-CC, 1877, 1877-CC, 1878-CC, 1879-CC, 1879-O, and 1883-O.

Indian Head $10 (1907–1933). Scarcer dates include 1920-S, 1930-S, and 1933.

Liberty Head $20 (1849–1907). Scarcer dates include 1854-O, 1856-O, 1859-O, 1860-O, 1861-O, 1861 (Tall Letters), 1861-S (Tall Letters), 1866-S, 1870-CC, 1871-CC, 1872-CC, 1873-CC, 1879-O, 1881, 1882, 1885, 1885-CC, 1886, 1891, and 1891-CC.

Saint-Gaudens $20 (1907–1933). Scarcer dates include the 1907 issues with Roman numerals (MCMVII), 1920-S, 1921, 1926-D, 1927-D, 1927-S, 1928, 1929, 1930-S, 1931, 1931-D, 1932, and the extremely rare 1933.

TYPICAL VALUES FOR U.S. GOLD COINS

These are prices you'll typically see for the most common dates of each major type of gold coin, in various conditions.

GOLD DOLLARS	F-12	VF-20	EF-40	MS-60	MS-63	MS-65	PF-63	PF-65
Liberty Head, Type 1, 1849–1854	$220	$225	$325	$425	$1,100	$4,250		
Princess, Type 2, 1854–1856	325	350	500	1,850	8,000	26,500	$150,000	$325,000
Princess, Type 3, 1856–1889	235	250	285	375	900	2,000	5,500	12,000

QUARTER EAGLES	F-12	VF-20	EF-40	MS-60	MS-63	MS-65	PF-63	PF-65
Capped Bust Right, No Stars, 1796	$42,500	$65,000	$92,500	$225,000	$475,000	$1,600,000		
Capped Bust Right, 1796–1807	5,250	8,250	13,000	32,500	75,000	300,000	$150,000	$325,000
Capped Bust Left, Large, 1808	30,000	45,000	60,000	150,000	375,000	525,000+	5,500	12,000
Capped Head Left, Large, 1821–1827	6,250	8,250	10,500	32,500	60,000		250,000	
Capped Head Left, Small, 1829–1834	5,500	6,500	8,500	23,000	35,000	85,000	100,000	150,000

QUARTER EAGLES	F-12	VF-20	EF-40	MS-60	MS-63	MS-65	PF-63	PF-65
Classic Head, 1834–1839	$350	$600	$850	$3,500	$11,500	$45,000	$100,000	$225,000
Liberty Head, 1840–1907	320	325	350	500	800	1,650	7,000	19,000
Indian Head, 1908–1929	265	275	300	400	725	2,650	8,500	25,000

THREE-DOLLAR GOLD PIECES	F-12	VF-20	EF-40	MS-60	MS-63	MS-65	PF-63	PF-65
Indian Princess Head, 1854–1889	$825	$850	$1,200	$2,550	$4,750	$15,000	$12,500	$32,500

HALF EAGLES	F-12	VF-20	EF-40	MS-60	MS-63	MS-65	PF-63	PF-65
Capped Bust, Small Eagle, 1795–1798	$18,000	$23,500	$28,500	$70,000	$150,000	$525,000	$12,500	$32,500
Capped Bust, Large Eagle, 1795–1807	4,000	5,000	7,000	15,000	28,000	120,000		
Capped Bust Left, Large, 1807–1812	3,000	4,000	5,000	13,500	25,000	95,000		
Capped Head, 1813–1834	5,000	6,750	8,000	17,500	35,000	150,000		
Classic Head, 1834–1838	650	675	900	4,500	11,500	55,000	85,000	200,000
Liberty Head, No Motto, 1839–1866	480	500	525	1,350	7,500	30,000	32,500	77,500
Liberty Head, 1866–1908	460	475	485	575	675	2,750	12,000	30,000
Indian Head, 1908–1929	470	480	485	625	2,000	15,000	12,000	35,000

EAGLES	F-12	VF-20	EF-40	MS-60	MS-63	MS-65	PF-63	PF-65
Caped Bust, Small Eagle, 1795–1797	$27,500	$35,000	$42,500	$95,000	$275,000	$500,000	$12,500	$32,500
Capped Bust, Large Eagle, 1797–1804	8,750	11,000	15,000	31,000	60,000	110,000		
Liberty Head, No Motto, 1838–1866	950	975	1,000	3,250	13,000	75,000	40,000	125,000
Liberty Head, 1866–1907	880	900	925	950	1,175	3,750	13,500	45,000
Indian Head, No Motto, 1907–1908	880	900	925	950	3,250	9,500	85,000	200,000
Indian Head, 1908–1933	880	900	925	950	1,350	3,500	15,500	50,000

DOUBLE EAGLES	F-12	VF-20	EF-40	MS-60	MS-63	MS-65	PF-63	PF-65
Liberty Head, No Motto, 1849–1866	$1,800	$1,850	$1,900	$4,200	$9,000	$25,000	$85,000	$300,000
Liberty Head, 1866–1876	1,800	1,850	1,875	1,950	12,000		50,000	170,000
Liberty Head, 1877–1907	1,800	1,825	1,850	1,875	2,075	3,750	30,000	85,000
Saint-Gaudens, Roman Numerals, High Relief, 1907	9,500	10,000	11,500	16,500	23,500	45,000	32,500	75,500
Saint-Gaudens, 1907–1933	1,800	1,825	1,850	1,900	1,975	2,350	30,000	75,000

19
COMMEMORATIVE
COINS

Commemorative coins have been popular since the time of ancient Greece and Rome. In the beginning they recorded and honored important events, and passed along the news of the day. Today commemorative coins, which are highly esteemed by collectors, have been issued by many modern nations. None of them has surpassed the United States when it comes to these impressive mementos.

The first U.S. commemorative coins were made to celebrate the World's Columbian Exposition, held in Chicago in 1893, and to honor Columbus's discovery of America under the patronage of Queen Isabella of Spain. The Columbian half dollar is one of the most commonly encountered classic commemoratives; many were unsold at the time of issue and were later released into circulation at face value. The 1892 version is worth $19 in AU-50, and the 1893 worth $17. The Isabella quarter is much scarcer, and is worth $475 in AU.

Commemorative coins illustrate the progress of people in the New World in an interesting and instructive manner. They artistically present a record of history that appeals strongly to the collector who favors the romantic, *storytelling* side of numismatics. Many Americans who would otherwise have little interest in coins, and would not otherwise consider themselves collectors, are drawn to the historical features of commemoratives.

These special coins are usually issued either to commemorate events or to help pay for monuments, programs, or celebrations that honor historical persons, places, or things. Before 1982, commemorative coins were offered in most instances by a commission in charge of the event to be commemorated, and sold at a premium over face value.

Popular ways to collect commemorative coins are by major types or in sets with mintmark varieties. They are sometimes grouped into the "classic" era (1892 to 1954) and the "modern" era (1982 to date). All commemoratives are of the standard weight and fineness of their regular-issue 20th-century gold and silver counterparts, and all are legal tender. One modern commemorative (the 2000 Library of Congress bicentennial $10) was minted in a special bimetallic composition of gold and platinum. Many modern half dollar commemoratives are copper-nickel instead of silver.

In recent years in particular, commemoratives have entered the broader awareness of the general public, outside of the coin-collecting community. In years past they were popular with collectors who enjoyed their artistry and history, as well as the potential to profit from owning these uncommon coins. Among the classic commemoratives, very few ever reached circulation (because they were all originally sold above face value), and because they are all so rare. But from time to time some did get spent like regular coins, especially if an issue didn't sell out and ended up being released into circulation at face value. Most of the early issues were half dollars, and they were often made in quantities of fewer than 20,000 pieces. This is minuscule when compared to regular coins that are made by the millions each year.

Historically, classic commemorative coins have frequently undergone a roller-coaster cycle of price adjustments. These cycles usually are short-lived, lasting from months to years, with prices always recovering and eventually exceeding previous levels.

Most modern-day commemoratives have stayed at or near their issue-price value, or risen in value very slowly. Some, however, have sold out quickly and developed a strong after-market; the 2001 American Buffalo commemorative is an example.

Alabama Centennial, 1921
Albany, NY, Charter, 1936
American Independence, 1926
Antietam, Battle of, 1937
Arkansas Centennial, 1935–1939
Bald Eagle, 2008
Bill of Rights, 1993

Black Revolutionary War Patriots, 1998
Booker T. Washington. See Washington, Booker T.
Boone, Daniel, 1934–1938
Botanic Garden, 1997
Boy Scouts, 2010

Braille, Louis, 2009
Bridgeport, CT, Centennial, 1936
Buffalo, American, 2001
California Diamond Jubilee, 1925
California Pacific International
  Exposition, 1935–1936
Capitol, U.S., 1994
Capitol Visitor Center, 2001
Carver, George Washington,
  1951–1954
Cincinnati Music Center, 1936
Civil War Battlefields, 1995
Cleveland / Great Lakes Exposition,
  1936
Columbia, SC, Sesquicentennial,
  1936
Columbian Exposition, 1892–1893
Columbus, Christopher, 1992
Congress Bicentennial, 1989
Congress, Library of, 2000
Connecticut Tercentenary, 1935
Constitution Bicentennial, 1987
Delaware Tercentenary, 1936
Disabled Veterans, 2010
Edison, Thomas A., 2004
Eisenhower Centennial, 1990
Elgin, IL, Centennial, 1936
Ericson, Leif, Millennium, 2000
First Flight Centennial, 2003
Fort Vancouver Centennial, 1925
Franklin, Benjamin, 2006
Gettysburg, Battle of, 1936
Grant Memorial, 1922
Hawaiian Sesquicentennial, 1928
Hudson, NY, Sesquicentennial, 1935
Huguenot-Walloon Tercentenary,
  1924
Illinois Centennial, 1918
Infantry Soldier, 2012
Iowa Centennial, 1946
Isabella Quarter Dollar, 1893
Jamestown 400th Anniversary, 2007
Jefferson, Thomas, 1993 (1994)
Kennedy, Robert F., 1998
Korean War Memorial, 1991

Lafayette Dollar, 1900
Lewis and Clark Bicentennial, 2004
Lewis and Clark Exposition,
  1904–1905
Lexington-Concord
  Sesquicentennial, 1925
Library of Congress Bicentennial,
  2000
Lincoln, Abraham, Bicentennial,
  2009
Little Rock Desegregation, 2007
Long Island Tercentenary, 1936
Louisiana Purchase Exposition, 1903
Lynchburg, VA, Sesquicentennial,
  1936
Madison, Dolley, 1999
Maine Centennial, 1920
Marine Corps 230th Anniversary,
  2005
Marshall, John, 2005
Maryland Tercentenary, 1934
McKinley Memorial, 1916–1917
Medal of Honor, 2011
Missouri Centennial, 1921
Monroe Doctrine Centennial, 1923
Mt. Rushmore Golden Anniversary,
  1991
National Law Enforcement Officers,
  1997
National Community Service, 1996
National Prisoners of War, 1994
New Rochelle, NY, 250th
  Anniversary, 1938
Norfolk, VA, Bicentennial, 1936
Old Spanish Trail, 1935
Olympics:
  1983–1984 (Los Angeles)
  1988 (Seoul)
  1992 (XXV/25th)
  1995 (Centennial)
  2002 (Salt Lake City)
Oregon Trail Memorial, 1926–1939
Panama-Pacific Exposition, 1915
Pilgrim Tercentenary, 1920–1921
Police Memorial, 1997

P.O.W.s, U.S., 1994
Providence, RI, Tercentenary, 1936
Roanoke Island, NC, 350th
    Anniversary, 1937
Robinson, Jackie, 1997
Robinson–Arkansas Centennial, 1936
Roosevelt, Franklin D., 1997
San Francisco Old Mint Centennial,
    2006
San Francisco–Oakland Bay Bridge,
    1936
Shriver / Special Olympics, 1995
Smithsonian 150th Anniversary, 1996
Spanish Trail, Old, 1935
Special Olympics, 1995
Star-Spangled Banner, 2012
Statue of Liberty Centennial, 1986
Stone Mountain Memorial, 1925
Texas Centennial, 1934–1938
U.S. Army, 2011
U.S. Capitol Bicentennial, 1994

United Service Organizations, 1991
Vermont Sesquicentennial, 1927
Vietnam Veterans, 1994
Washington, Booker T., 1946–1951;
    1951–1954
Washington, George, 1982
  Bicentennial of Death, 1999
West Point Bicentennial, 2002
White House 200th Anniversary,
    1992
Wisconsin Territorial Centennial,
    1936
Women in Military Service, 1994
World Cup (Soccer) Tournament,
    1994
World War II 50th Anniversary,
    1991–1995
World War II, 1993
Yellowstone National Park, 1999
York County, ME, Tercentenary,
    1936

The 1900 Lafayette silver dollar honored George Washington
and General Lafayette, the French hero of the American
Revolution. The coin is worth $650 in AU-50 condition.

This octagonal $50
gold commemora-
tive coin was
struck for the
1915 Panama-
Pacific Expo-
sition in San
Francisco.
Only 645
were sold at
the time;
today they're
worth more than
$47,000 in AU-50.

The 1923 Monroe Doctrine Centennial half dollar is another that saw poor sales, and many unsold coins were released into circulation at face value. Today they're often found in circulated grades. An AU-50 example is worth about $65.

Only the second commemorative to pass the 1 million mark in mintage, the 1925 Stone Mountain Memorial half dollar is relatively common today. An MS-60 example can be had for about $60.

A famous rarity among classic commemoratives is the 1928 Hawaiian Sesquicentennial half dollar. Just over 10,000 were sold at an issue price of $2 each—the highest up to that time. Today that $2 investment is worth $1,700 in About Uncirculated, and from $2,500 to $11,500 or more in Mint State.

The San Francisco – Oakland Bay Bridge Opening half dollar of 1936 had a relatively high distribution of 71,424 coins. Today an AU-50 example is worth $170, with lower-end Mint State examples worth an additional $10 to $50.

The Booker T. Washington Memorial half dollar was produced from 1946 to 1951, at the Philadelphia, Denver, and San Francisco mints. It was issued to perpetuate the ideals and teachings of the famous educator and to construct memorials in his honor. As a type, these coins are fairly common, and are worth $16 to $25 in AU to lower-end Mint State grades.

The Booker T. Washington / Washington Carver half dollar of 1951 to 1954 was struck to promote "freedom and opportunity for all" and to raise money "to oppose the spread of communism among Negroes in the interest of national defense." These commemoratives are relatively common, and worth between $16 and $24 in AU and lower-end Mint State grades.

There was a nearly 30-year hiatus after the last commemorative coins of the 1950s were minted, as Congress felt the program had been abused by special interests and poor planning. Finally, in 1982, the commemorative program was revived with a smashing success: the George Washington half dollar, honoring the 250th anniversary of the president's birth. Today these popular silver coins are worth $15 in Mint State and $16 in Proof.

The 1986 Statue of Liberty Centennial coins were another popular hit for the U.S. Mint. Millions of the coins were sold in Proof and Mint State formats: a copper-nickel half dollar (worth $6 today in either format), a silver dollar (worth $36), and a gold $5 coin (worth $475).

Baseball legend Jackie Robinson was honored for his legacy of courage with a 1997 silver dollar and gold $5 coin. Today the silver dollar is worth $85 to $100. The gold piece, meanwhile, has skyrocketed to $650 in Proof, or $3,600 in Mint State!

The 2001 American Buffalo silver dollar, made to raise money for the Smithsonian's cultural exhibits, quickly sold out its authorized mintage. This hugely popular coin, with its design based on the 1913–1938 Buffalo nickel, is worth $200 today.

Many significant military, political, and cultural themes have been celebrated on recent half dollars, silver dollars, and $5 gold coins. The U.S. Mint produces new commemorative coins every year, offering collectors an exciting variety to pick from.

20

PROOF AND MINT SETS

The U.S. Mint has a long tradition of producing sets of Proof coins and Uncirculated coins, packaged for sale to collectors.

Very few Proof coins—specimen strikings made for presentation, souvenir, exhibition, or collecting—were made prior to 1856. Such coins are rare, and infrequently sold (compared to coins struck for circulation). See chapter 4 to learn how Proof coins are made.

The modern era of Proof sets started in 1936. Proof coins were struck at the Philadelphia Mint from 1936 to 1942. In 1942, when the composition of the nickel changed to include silver, there were two types of the five-cent coin available to collectors, and both were packaged in Proof sets.

Proof coin production was temporarily suspended from 1943 through 1949, during World War II and for several years following. It was suspended again from 1965 through 1967 (although "Special Mint Sets" were produced during those years). Regular Proof sets were resumed in 1968.

The U.S. Mint issues annual sets of Proof coins, as well as Uncirculated coins, in special packaging for collectors.

Sets from 1936 through 1972 include the cent, nickel, dime, quarter, and half dollar. From 1973 through 1981 the dollar coin was added. Regular Proof sets issued from 1982 to 1998 contain the cent through half dollar. From 1983 through 1997 the Mint also offered special Prestige Proof sets that included commemorative coins along with the year's regular Proofs. From 1999 to 2009, Proof sets included five different State quarters or six Territorial quarters. 1999 Proof dollars were sold separately. From 2000 to date the sets have again included dollar coins. And since 2007 four-coin Presidential dollar sets have also been issued.

These are the values for Proof sets in average unspotted condition and (after 1955) in original government packaging.

PROOF SETS	Current Value
1936	$7,500
1937	4,250
1938	2,000
1939	1,850
1940	1,500
1941	1,500
1942, Both nickels	1,400
1942, One nickel	1,300
1950	700
1951	675
1952	275
1953	240
1954	115
1955, Box pack	125
1955, Flat pack	150
1956	50
1957	30
1958	40
1959	30
1960, With Large Date cent	30
1960, With Small Date cent	38

PROOF SETS	Current Value
1961	$28.00
1962	28.00
1963	28.00
1964	28.00
1968S	8.00
1968S, With No S dime	16,000.00
1969S	8.00
1970S	9.00
1970S, With Small Date cent	100.00
1970S, With No S dime	1,000.00
1971S	6.00
1971S, With No S nickel	1,400.00
1972S	7.00
1973S	8.50
1974S	9.00
1975S, With 1976 quarter, half, and dollar	9.00
1975S, With No S dime	—
1976S	8.00
1976S, Silver clad, 3-piece set	25.00

PROOF SETS	Current Value		PROOF SETS	Current Value
1977S	$7.50		1990S, With No S cent (Prestige set)	$5,800
1978S	8.00		1990S, Prestige set (Eisenhower dollar)	38
1979S, Type 1	8.00			
1979S, Type 2	85.00		1991S	8
1980S	7.00		1991S, Prestige set (Mt. Rushmore half, dollar)	56
1981S, Type 1	8.00			
1981S, Type 2 (all six coins in set)	325.00		1992S	6
			1992S, Prestige set (Olympic half, dollar)	55
1982S	5.00		1992S, Silver	30
1983S	6.00		1992S, Silver Premier set	32
1983S, With No S dime	1,000.00		1993S	9
1983S, Prestige set (Olympic dollar)	50.00		1993S, Prestige set (Bill of Rights half, dollar)	60
1984S	6.00			
1984S, Prestige set (Olympic dollar)	50.00		1993S, Silver	35
			1993S, Silver Premier set	37
1985S	6.00		1994S	9
1986S	6.00		1994S, Prestige set (World Cup half, dollar)	45
1986S, Prestige set (Statue of Liberty half, dollar)	38.00			
			1994S, Silver	30
1987S	5.00		1994S, Silver Premier set	32
1987S, Prestige set (Constitution dollar)	38.00		1995S	16
			1995S, Prestige set (Civil War half, dollar)	90
1988S	7.00			
1988S, Prestige set (Olympic dollar)	38.00		1995S, Silver	60
			1995S, Silver Premier set	70
1989S	7.00		1996S	10
1989S, Prestige set (Congressional half, dollar)	38.00		1996S, Prestige set (Olympic half, dollar)	300
1990S	7.00		1996S, Silver	30
1990S, With No S cent	5,800.00		1996S, Silver Premier set	32

PROOF SETS	Current Value
1997S	$15
1997S, Prestige set (Botanic dollar)	85
1997S, Silver	45
1997S, Silver Premier set	50
1998S	11
1998S, Silver	28
1998S, Silver Premier set	30
1999S, 9-piece set	15
1999S, 5-piece quarter set	12
1999S, Silver 9-piece set	135
2000S, 10-piece set	8
2000S, 5-piece quarter set	6
2000S, Silver 10-piece set	65
2001S, 10-piece set	20
2001S, 5-piece quarter set	12
2001S, Silver 10-piece set	70
2002S, 10-piece set	15
2002S, 5-piece quarter set	10
2002S, Silver 10-piece set	60
2003S, 10-piece set	12
2003S, 5-piece quarter set	7
2003S, Silver 10-piece set	60
2004S, 11-piece set	12
2004S, 5-piece quarter set	7
2004S, Silver 11-piece set	60
2004S, Silver 5-piece quarter set	40
2005S, 11-piece set	8
2005S, 5-piece quarter set	7

PROOF SETS	Current Value
2005S, Silver 11-piece set	$60
2005S, Silver 5-piece quarter set	35
2006S, 10-piece set	12
2006S, 5-piece quarter set	9
2006S, Silver 10-piece set	60
2006S, Silver 5-piece quarter set	35
2007S, 14-piece set	12
2007S, 5-piece quarter set	9
2007S, 4-piece Presidential set	10
2007S, Silver 14-piece set	62
2007S, Silver 5-piece quarter set	36
2008S, 14-piece set	75
2008S, 5-piece quarter set	35
2008S, 4-piece Presidential set	15
2008S, Silver 14-piece set	75
2008S, Silver 5-piece quarter set	35
2009S, 18-piece set	25
2009S, 6-piece quarter set	20
2009S, 4-piece Presidential set	20
2009S, Silver 18-piece set	70
2009S, Silver 6-piece quarter set	45
2009S, 4-piece Lincoln Bicentennial set	20
2010S, 14-piece set	38
2010S, 5-piece quarter set	18

PROOF SETS	Current Value
2010S, 4-piece Presidential set	$20
2010S, Silver 14-piece set	60
2010S, Silver 5-piece quarter set	35
2011S, 14-piece set	38

PROOF SETS	Current Value
2011S, 5-piece quarter set	$18
2011S, 4-piece Presidential set	25
2011S, Silver 14-piece set	75
2011S, Silver 5-piece quarter set	42

Starting in the 1940s, official Uncirculated Mint sets have been specially packaged by the Mint for sale to collectors. They contain Uncirculated specimens of each year's coins for every denomination issued from each mint. In the early years, the coins were the same as those normally intended for circulation and were not minted with any special consideration for quality. From 2005 through 2010, Mint sets were made with a satin finish rather than the traditional Uncirculated luster.

Uncirculated Mint sets sold by the Treasury from 1947 through 1958 contained two examples of each regular-issue coin. These were packaged in cardboard holders that did not protect the coins from tarnish. Nicely preserved sets generally command stronger prices. No official Uncirculated Mint sets were produced in 1950, 1982, or 1983.

Since 1959, sets have been sealed in protective plastic envelopes.

UNCIRCULATED MINT SETS	Current Value
1947 P-D-S	$1,500
1948 P-D-S	775
1949 P-D-S	1,000
1951 P-D-S	950
1952 P-D-S	850
1953 P-D-S	600
1954 P-D-S	275
1955 P-D-S	180
1956 P-D	175
1957 P-D	285
1958 P-D	150
1959 P-D	65
1960 P-D	55

UNCIRCULATED MINT SETS	Current Value
1961 P-D	$60.00
1962 P-D	55.00
1963 P-D	55.00
1964 P-D	55.00
1968 P-D-S	7.50
1969 P-D-S	7.50
1970 P-D-S, With Large Date cent	13.00
1970 P-D-S, With Small Date cent	75.00
1971 P-D-S (no Eisenhower dollar)	4.00
1972 P-D-S (no Eisenhower dollar)	4.00
1973 P-D-S	12.00

UNCIRCULATED MINT SETS	Current Value		UNCIRCULATED MINT SETS	Current Value
1974 P-D-S	$8		1994 P-D	$7
1975 P-D, With 1976 quarter, half, dollar	7		1995 P-D	7
1776–1976, Silver clad, 3-piece set	25		1996 P-D, Plus 1996W dime	18
1976 P-D	7		1997 P-D	10
1977 P-D	9		1998 P-D	6
1978 P-D	8		1999 P-D (18 pieces) (dollar not included)	12
1979 P-D (S-mint dollar not included)	6		2000 P-D (20 pieces)	12
1980 P-D-S	8		2001 P-D (20 pieces)	16
1981 P-D-S	12		2002 P-D (20 pieces)	16
1984 P-D	5		2003 P-D (20 pieces)	16
1985 P-D	6		2004 P-D (22 pieces)	20
1986 P-D	10		2005 P-D (22 pieces)	12
1987 P-D	6		2006 P-D (20 pieces)	17
1988 P-D	7		2007 P-D (28 pieces)	20
1989 P-D	5		2008 P-D (28 pieces)	65
1990 P-D	5		2009 P-D (36 pieces)	35
1991 P-D	6		2010 P-D (28 pieces)	35
1992 P-D	6		2011 P-D (28 pieces)	35
1993 P-D	8			

Note: Uncirculated Mint Sets issued from 2005 through 2010 have a special Satin Finish that is somewhat different from the finish on Uncirculated coins made for general circulation.

In 1965, 1966, and 1967, "Special Mint Sets" of higher-than-normal quality, packaged in hard plastic holders, were made to substitute for Proof sets, which were not made during those years.

SPECIAL MINT SETS	Current Value
1965	$11
1966	11
1967	12

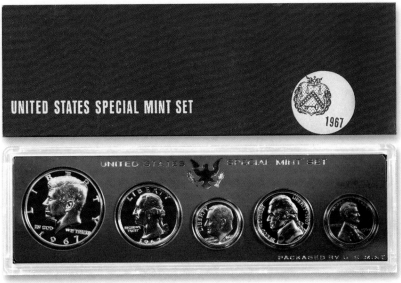

1967 Special Mint Set.

Uncirculated Souvenir sets were packaged and sold in gift shops at the Philadelphia and Denver mints in 1982 and 1983 in place of the official Mint sets, which were not made in those years. A bronze Mint medal is packaged with each set. Similar sets were also made in other years.

SOUVENIR SETS	Current Value
1982P	$65
1982D	65
1983P	100
1983D	80

21
SILVER, GOLD, AND PLATINUM BULLION

The United States entered the international gold-and-silver bullion market in 1986 when it launched its multiple-coin American Eagle program. Since then the U.S. Mint has branched out with many innovative bullion products to meet the worldwide demand—from collectors and investors alike—for high-quality silver, gold, and platinum.

The U.S. Mint's modern bullion coin program started under President Ronald Reagan, in 1986.

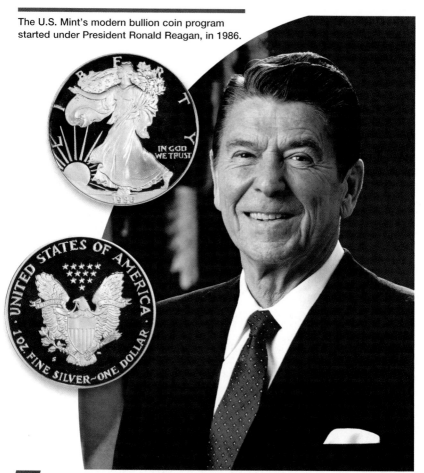

In addition to regular bullion strikes (normal Uncirculated coins, for investment), the Mint offers its bullion coins in various collectible formats, in smaller quantities. Coins with Proof, Reverse Proof, and Burnished finishes have been packaged in various sets and individually.

The American Silver Eagle is a one-ounce .9993 fine bullion coin with a face value of $1. On its obverse is Adolph A. Weinman's Liberty Walking design, used on half dollars from 1916 through 1947. The reverse is a rendition of a heraldic eagle by Mint engraver John M. Mercanti. More than 300 million of these coins have been sold since 1986! Values for regular bullion-strike coins are generally pegged to the current market price of silver. Special collector versions have additional value, and some are worth much more than their bullion content. Examples include the 2008-W, Burnished finish, Reverse of 2007 (worth about $400) . . . the 2001-S (worth about $250) . . . and several 2012 varieties. These coins are discussed in detail in John Mercanti's *American Silver Eagles: A Guide to the U.S. Bullion Coin Program.*

Since 2010 the Mint has been issuing large "America the Beautiful" silver bullion coins in conjunction with the quarter dollars of the same series. Each coin is three inches in diameter and contains an impressive five ounces of .999 fine silver. Both regular-issue bullion coins and special-finish collector coins are offered.

The weight and purity of the America the Beautiful
silver bullion coins are incused on the edge.

The American Gold Eagle program includes four denominations of 1 ounce, 1/2 ounce, 1/4 ounce, and 1/10 ounce of .9167 fine gold. The obverse has a modified rendition of the Augustus Saint-Gaudens design used on U.S. $20 gold pieces from 1907 to 1933. The reverse displays a "family of eagles" motif by artist Miley Tucker-Frost. Like the Silver Eagles, these gold coins are sold as investments and also in several collector formats and packages.

Two examples of American Gold Eagles: the
one-ounce $50 coin, and the tenth-ounce $5.

American Buffalo gold bullion coins, minted since 2006, were the first .9999 fine (24-karat) gold coins made by the U.S. Mint. They're produced at its West Point facility. In 2006 and 2007, only one-ounce coins (with a $50 face value) were minted. In 2008 the Mint also produced half-ounce ($25 face value), quarter-ounce ($10), and tenth-ounce ($5) pieces in Proof and Uncirculated formats, individually and in sets. Like other gold bullion coins, their values change frequently and are based on prevailing bullion and fabrication costs relative to the weight of each denomination.

American Buffalo .9999 fine gold bullion.

First Spouse bullion coins, also made in .9999 fine gold, debuted in 2007. They weigh one-half ounce and have a face value of $10, which of course is much lower than their bullion value. The coins honor the nation's first spouses on the same schedule as the Mint's Presidential dollar program. Each features a portrait on the obverse, and on the reverse a unique design symbolic of the spouse's life and work. In instances where a president held office without a spouse, the coin bears "an obverse image emblematic of Liberty as depicted on a circulating coin of that era and a reverse image emblematic of themes of that president's life."

Various First Spouse
.9999 fine gold
bullion coins.

The Philadelphia Mint in 2009 produced a modern version of the famous 1907 Ultra High Relief double eagle gold pattern coin. It was made as a tour de force to demonstrate how technical advances in minting techniques can now accommodate manufacturing such a coin. The original 1907 design was never made for commercial use because at the time it was impossible to produce in sufficient quantities. The 2009 coins (4 mm thick and containing one ounce of .9999 fine gold) were made at West Point and packaged in a special mahogany box. More than 114,000 were purchased, and each is worth $2,600 to $3,700 today, depending on grade.

The MMIX (2009) Ultra High Relief gold coin, photographed at an angle
to show the edge (lettered E PLURIBUS UNUM) and the depth of relief.

In 2007 the Mint launched a new precious metal in its bullion program: platinum. Four coins make up the series, in face values of $100 (one ounce), $50 (half ounce), $25 (quarter ounce), and $10 (tenth ounce). The main bullion design for these .9995 fine coins is a close-up view of the Statue of Liberty, and an eagle soaring in flight. As with the silver and gold programs, the Mint has offered the platinum coins in several special formats and finishes for collectors. The collectible Proof one-ounce versions have featured various designs in the "Vistas of Liberty" and "Foundations of Democracy" series.

Two examples of American Platinum Eagles: the
half-ounce $50 coin, and the tenth-ounce $10.

Several of the collectible one-ounce platinum Proofs, from the
"Vistas of Liberty" and "Foundations of Democracy" series.

22
TOKENS AND MEDALS

If you've found some coin-like objects in Grandpa's cigar box—small, round copper, nickel, or silver pieces that *look* like coins, but aren't illustrated or described elsewhere in this book—you might have a token a medal. *Exonumia* is a word that covers the study and collecting of these objects.

What exactly are tokens and medals? In the *Guide Book of United States Tokens and Medals,* historian Katherine Jaeger writes, "Medals have been issued to commemorate historic events, to serve as souvenirs of a location or occasion, to honor important individuals, to be offered as diplomatic gifts, and strictly for art's sake." Medals are struck by private studios, by commercial mints, and sometimes even by the U.S. Mint itself. Tokens, meanwhile, are similar to medals but fundamentally different. "Tokens . . . were issued as substitutes for money, to be used as a medium of exchange, and as such they do not often bear heavy symbolism or carry profound meanings. Tokens advertised the shops of merchants, carried patriotic or political messages, paid for shows, games, and rides, and even took the place of coins when national economic conditions created coin shortages."

Medals and tokens have long been collected as part of American numismatics—going back to the 1700s. Pictured are U.S. Assay medals from 1901 and 1904.

Millions of tokens and medals have been produced in the United States. Jaeger breaks them down into the following groups, each covered in detail in her book:

Tokens of exchange, accounting, and advertising—These include merchant tokens, Hard Times tokens (1832–1844), Civil War tokens (1860–1865), company store and commissary tokens, amusement tokens, gaming chips and tokens, transportation tokens, and government-sponsored tokens.

Souvenir and commemorative medals and tokens—These include contemporary medals and tokens, exposition souvenirs, and personal medals and tokens. Jaeger gives special focus to the historical commemorative "craze" of 1858 to 1861, and coin medals of the Franklin Mint.

Political and presidential exonumia—These include presidential campaign medals and tokens, political-cause pieces, inaugural medals, Indian Peace medals, and post-presidency commemoratives.

Art medals—This category includes art and exhibition medals.

Prize medals—Academic medals, major institutional medals, fair and exposition medals, and lifesaving and heroism medals are in this category.

Fraternal and membership-themed medals—This includes such things as firefighters' medals, military and other challenge coins, and incentive medals and tokens.

Hard Times tokens are generally about the size of a copper large cent. These were privately struck from 1832 to 1844, during a period of economic hardship and political strife in the United States. Hundreds of varieties were made, some with political messages and some advertising businesses. Most are very affordable, although there are some major rarities. Values, depending on the type, range from about $25 to $35 in Very Fine to hundreds or even thousands of dollars in the same grade.

Tooled and altered coins—This field includes merchant advertising on coins (countermarks, stickers, etc.), carved coins, elongated coins, love tokens, and engraved, enameled, cut-out, and pop-out coins.

Most modern mass-produced tokens and medals are worth anywhere from less than $1 up to several dollars apiece. Older pieces, and those struck in silver or gold, can be worth hundreds or even thousands of dollars.

The tokens and medals pictured here are some of the historical types most frequently seen in U.S. collections. You can learn more about them in the *Guide Book of United States Coins*, or in the aforementioned *Guide Book of United States Tokens and Medals*.

Civil War tokens are generally divided into two groups: tradesmen's tokens (also called store cards), and anonymously issued pieces with political or patriotic themes. These were privately struck during the Civil War, mostly in 1863, to make up for the lack of government-issued cents in circulation. (Americans hoarded all federal coinage, from gold and silver down to bronze cents, uncertain what the outcome of the war would bring.) An estimated 50 million or more Civil War tokens were issued by various companies and private individuals. Some 10,000 different varieties have been recorded. In general, copper or brass tokens are worth $15 to $100 (Fine to Mint State) . . . nickel tokens are worth $60 to $250 (same grades) . . . white metal tokens, $80 to $225 . . . copper-nickel, $75 to $300 . . . and silver, $200 to $1,200. Of course, certain scarce and rare tokens can be worth more—hundreds or thousands of dollars. Those from Alabama, Washington, D.C., Louisiana, Maryland, Minnesota, Tennessee, and Virginia are generally the most valuable.

23
UNITED STATES / PHILIPPINES COINS

It's not uncommon to find a stash of mementoes from a relative's travels, and among them discover unusual old coins that appear to be a hybrid of American and foreign. You'll see the familiar words UNITED STATES OF AMERICA, and an American eagle and shield, but the denominations are centavos and pesos, and the design elements are exotic. Are these coins U.S. money? In a way, yes—but they were made many years ago, for a land 8,500 miles away from the American capital.

In this detail from an 1898 political cartoon, Uncle Sam welcomes the world's merchants into the Philippine Islands, newly liberated from Spanish imperial control. To facilitate trade the United States would soon begin minting coins and printing paper money for the islands.

In 1899 the United States acquired the Philippine Islands as part of a treaty with Spain, ending the Spanish-American War of 1898. The U.S. military suppressed a Filipino insurgency through 1902, and partway through that struggle, in 1901, replaced the military government with a civil administration. One of its first tasks was to sponsor new coinage that would be compatible with the old Spanish system while also exchangeable for American money, at the rate of two Philippine pesos to the U.S. dollar.

The resulting coins, struck at the Philadelphia and San Francisco mints, were introduced in 1903. They bear the identities of both the Philippines (*Filipinas* in Spanish) and the United States of America. Following Spanish custom, the peso was divided into 100 centavos. A dollar-sized coin valued at one peso was the principal issue in this series, but silver fractions were also minted in values of 50, 20, and 10 centavos. Minor coinage included the copper-nickel 5-cent piece, as well as 1-centavo and 1/2-centavo coins of bronze.

This peso (shown actual size) illustrates the basic design used on the Philippines' silver coins minted under U.S. sovereignty up to 1935. The 5-centavos coin (shown enlarged) illustrates the motif used on the smaller-denomination bronze and copper-nickel pieces. The designs were by Filipino engraver Melecio Figueroa.

A rise in the price of silver forced the reduction of the fineness and weight for each silver denomination beginning in 1907, and subsequent issues are smaller in diameter. The smaller size of the new silver coins led to confusion between the silver 20-centavo piece and the copper-nickel 5-centavo piece, resulting in a mismatching of coinage dies for these two denominations (an error that occurred in 1918 and again in 1928). A solution was found by reducing the diameter of the 5-centavo coin beginning in 1930.

In 1935 an act of Congress established the Commonwealth of the Philippines, and the following year a three-piece set of commemorative coins was issued to mark this transition. Despite the popularity of U.S. commemoratives at that time, the sets sold poorly, and thousands remained within the Philippine Treasury at the onset of World War II.

The commonwealth arms, introduced on the 1936 commemorative coins, were adapted to all circulating issues beginning in 1937.

The commemorative coins of 1936, marking the establishment of the Commonwealth of the Philippines, featured the new coat of arms on the reverse.

In 1942 the fast advance on the Philippines by Japanese forces prompted authorities to remove much of the Treasury's bullion to the United States. More than 15 million pesos' worth of silver stayed behind, mostly in the form of one-peso coins dated 1907 through 1912, plus many of the unsold 1936 commemoratives. The coins were hastily crated and dumped into Manila's Caballo Bay to prevent their capture. After the Japanese seized the Philippines, they learned about the submerged coins and managed to salvage some 4 million of them. Following the war American and Philippine treasure hunters pulled more of the coins up from the sea. By then many of them were badly corroded by the saltwater; this has contributed to the present-day scarcity of high-grade pre-war silver coins.

Philippine coins dated from 1903 to 1919 were struck at the Philadelphia and San Francisco mints. Those dated after 1920 were made in Manila at a branch of the U.S. Mint there. During World War II, coins of 1944 and 1945 were made at Philadelphia, Denver, and San Francisco.

The Philippines became an independent republic on July 4, 1946, ending a historic and colorful chapter in the history of U.S. coinage.

The following are prices you'll typically see for the most common dates of Philippine coins struck under U.S. sovereignty and as a commonwealth. For more detailed information, including values for every date, consult the annually issued *Guide Book of United States Coins* (the "Red Book").

U.S. SOVEREIGNTY ISSUES	VF	EF	MS-60	MS-63	Proof
1/2 centavo, 17.5 mm, 1903–1908		$2.00	$15	$40	$175
1 centavo, 24 mm, 1903–1936	$1.25	2.50	20	50	550
5 centavos, 20.5 mm, 1903–1928	1.50	2.50	20	35	60
5 centavos, 19 mm, 1930–1935	2.50	5.00	50	125	55
10 centavos, 17.5 mm, 1903–1906	3.00	6.00	35	75	110
10 centavos, 16.5 mm, 1907–1935	1.75	3.00	20	50	250
20 centavos, 23 mm, 1903–1906	5.00	8.00	45	100	
20 centavos, 20 mm, 1907–1929	3.00	4.00	25	75	275
50 centavos, 30 mm, 1903–1906	15.00	17.50	70	120	175
50 centavos, 27 mm, 1907–1921	8.00	9.00	35	75	375
1 peso, 38 mm, 1903–1906	28.00	30.00	125	200	325
1 peso, 35 mm, 1907–1912	18.00	20.00	100	225	800

COMMONWEALTH ISSUES	VF	EF	MS–60	MS–63
1 centavo, 1937–1944	$0.25	$0.75	$2.00	$5.00
5 centavos, 1937–1945	0.25	0.50	1.00	2.50
10 centavos, 1937–1945	1.25	1.50	2.50	5.00
20 centavos, 1937–1945	3.00	3.25	3.50	5.00
50 centavos, 1944–1945	8.00	9.00	10.00	12.00

COMMEMORATIVE ISSUES	VF	EF	MS–60	MS–63
50 centavos, 1936M	$25	$50.00	$10.00	$150
1 peso, 1936M, Murphy/Quezon	60	85.00	150.00	250
1 peso, 1936M, Roosevelt/Quezon	60	85.00	150.00	250
20 centavos, 1937–1945	3	3.25	3.50	5
50 centavos, 1944–1945	8	9.00	10.00	12

24
MISSTRIKES AND ERROR COINS

The U.S. Mint produces millions of coins each year, and it's natural that a few abnormal pieces escape inspection and are inadvertently released into circulation. These aren't considered regular issues because they're not made intentionally—but they have an enthusiastic following among coin collectors.

Errors are classified in general groups related to the kinds of manufacturing malfunctions involved. Nearly every error coin is unique in some way, and prices may vary from coin to coin. Collectors value these pieces according to their scarcity, and supply and demand.

Collectors eagerly seek misstruck and error coins— like this multiple-strike Indian Head cent (shown enlarged)—as a variation from normal date-and-mint series collecting.

These are just a few of the many kinds of error coins: A *clipped planchet* is an incomplete coin, missing 10 to 25 percent of its metal. A *multiple strike* is a coin with at least one additional image from being struck again off center. A *blank* or *planchet* is a blank disc of metal intended for coinage but not struck by dies. An *off-center* coin is one that has been struck out of collar and incorrectly centered, with part of the design missing. A *broadstrike* is a coin that was struck outside the coinage press's retaining collar. A *brockage* is a mirror image of the design impressed on the opposite side of the same coin.

The coins discussed in this chapter must not be confused with others that have been mutilated or damaged after leaving the mint. Examples of such pieces include coins that have been scratched, hammered, engraved, impressed, acid etched, or plated in order to simulate something other than a normal coin. Those pieces have no numismatic value, and can only be considered as altered coins not suitable for a collection.

An off-center Flying Eagle cent.

A Lincoln Memorial cent brockage.

A clipped-planchet Liberty Head nickel.

A broadstruck Jefferson nickel.

A multiple-strike State quarter.

A golden dollar planchet, with raised rim.

TYPICAL VALUES FOR ERROR COINS

The following are prices you'll typically see for various kinds of error coins. For more detailed information, consult the annually issued *Guide Book of United States Coins* (the "Red Book").

	Clipped Planchet	Multiple Strike	Planchet, Raised Rim	Off Center	Broad-strike	Brockage
Large Cent	$60	$900	$150.00	$500	$100	$850
Indian 1¢	20	700	—	150	60	400
Lincoln 1¢ (95% Copper)	4	60	3.00	10	8	35
Steel 1¢	18	250	40.00	75	40	200
Lincoln 1¢ (Zinc)	4	45	3.50	8	5	40
Liberty 5¢	30	700	30.00	200	125	400
Buffalo 5¢	40	2,500	20.00	450	250	1,000
Jefferson 5¢	4	60	10.00	12	10	50
Wartime 5¢	15	400	350.00	175	70	250
Barber 10¢	75	750	—	300	100	400
Mercury 10¢	25	800	—	175	75	275
Roosevelt 10¢ (Silver)	15	250	50.00	125	65	120
Roosevelt 10¢ (Clad)	4	50	3.50	10	10	50

	Clipped Planchet	Multiple Strike	Planchet, Raised Rim	Off Center	Broad-strike	Brockage
Washington 25¢ (Silver)	$20	$400	$100	$350	$200	$300
Washington 25¢ (Clad)	6	150	5	70	20	50
Bicentennial 25¢	40	350	—	150	50	250
Statehood 25¢	40	500	—	125	50	400
Franklin 50¢	40	1,800	—	1,500	450	650
Kennedy 50¢ (40% Silver)	30	1,200	135	450	250	450
Kennedy 50¢ (Clad)	25	600	100	200	100	300
Bicentennial 50¢	50	700	—	300	75	750
Silver $1	50	5,000	1,500	2,500	1,200	—
Eisenhower $1	50	1,350	100	700	175	1,200
Bicentennial $1	50	2,000	—	850	200	1,500
Anthony $1	35	800	120	300	75	300
Sacagawea $1	100	1,800	100	1,500	350	700

APPENDIX A

BULLION VALUES OF SILVER AND GOLD COINS

These charts show the bullion values of common-date circulated silver and gold U.S. coins. These are intrinsic values and do not reflect any numismatic premium a coin might have. The weight listed under each denomination is its actual silver weight (ASW) or actual gold weight (AGW).

BULLION VALUES OF SILVER COINS

In recent years, the bullion price of silver has fluctuated considerably. You can use the following chart to determine the approximate bullion value of many 19th- and 20th-century silver coins at various bullion-price levels. Or you can calculate the approximate value by multiplying the current spot price of silver (found online or in your daily newspaper) by the ASW for each coin, as indicated. Dealers generally purchase common silver coins at around 15 percent below bullion value, and sell them at around 15 percent above bullion value.

Silver Price Per Ounce	Wartime Nickel .05626 oz.	Dime .07234 oz.	Quarter .18084 oz.	Half Dollar .36169 oz.	Silver Clad Half Dollar .14792 oz.	Silver Dollar .77344 oz.
$28	$1.58	$2.03	$5.06	$10.13	$4.14	$21.66
29	1.63	2.10	5.24	10.49	4.29	22.43
30	1.69	2.17	5.43	10.85	4.44	23.20
31	1.74	2.24	5.61	11.21	4.59	23.98
32	1.80	2.31	5.79	11.57	4.73	24.75
33	1.86	2.39	5.97	11.94	4.88	25.52
34	1.91	2.46	6.15	12.30	5.03	26.30
35	1.97	2.53	6.33	12.66	5.18	27.07
36	2.03	2.60	6.51	13.02	5.33	27.84
37	2.08	2.68	6.69	13.38	5.47	28.62
38	2.14	2.75	6.87	13.74	5.62	29.39
39	2.19	2.82	7.05	14.11	5.77	30.16
40	2.25	2.89	7.23	14.47	5.92	30.94

Nearly all U.S. gold coins have an additional premium value beyond their bullion content, and thus are not subject to minor bullion-price variations. The premium amount is not necessarily tied to the bullion price of gold, but is usually determined by supply and demand levels in the numismatic marketplace. Because these factors can vary significantly, there is no reliable formula for calculating the "percentage below and above bullion prices" that would remain accurate over time. The gold chart here lists bullion values based on AGW only; consult a coin dealer to ascertain current buy and sell prices.

Gold Price Per Ounce	Half Dollar .36169 oz.	Silver Clad Half Dollar .14792 oz.	Silver Dollar .77344 oz.
$1,425	$344.66	$689.34	$1,378.69
1,450	350.71	701.44	1,402.88
1,475	356.76	713.53	1,427.06
1,500	362.81	725.63	1,451.25
1,525	368.85	737.72	1,475.44
1,550	374.90	749.81	1,499.63
1,575	380.95	761.91	1,523.81
1,600	386.99	774.00	1,548.00
1,625	393.04	786.09	1,572.19
1,650	399.09	798.19	1,596.38
1,675	405.13	810.28	1,620.56
1,700	411.18	822.38	1,644.75
1,725	417.23	834.47	1,668.94
1,750	423.27	846.56	1,693.13
1,775	429.32	858.66	1,717.31
1,800	435.37	870.75	1,741.50
1,825	441.41	882.84	1,765.69
1,850	447.46	894.94	1,789.88
1,875	453.51	907.03	1,814.06
1,900	459.55	919.13	1,838.25
1,925	465.60	931.22	1,862.44
1,950	471.65	943.31	1,886.63
1,975	477.69	955.41	1,910.81
2,000	483.74	967.50	1,935.00
2,025	489.79	979.59	1,959.19
2,050	495.83	991.69	1,983.38

APPENDIX B

FAMOUS COIN HOARDS AND TREASURES

In the 1960s and 1970s the U.S. government released a huge hoard of millions of silver dollars. When they hit the open market, the coins caused a sensation and an explosion of buying, selling, and collecting. That wasn't the first or only hoard of coins in U.S. history. Here are a few others that have attracted interest and attention over the years.

The Castine Hoard of Early Silver Coins. In late 1840, farmer Stephen Grindle and his son Samuel found a large old French silver coin near the Bagaduce River, about six miles from the harbor of Castine, Maine. A bit of digging unearthed more treasure. Between November 1840 and April 1841 they dug up hundreds of coins from Massachusetts, England, Holland, France, Portugal, Spain, and the Spanish colonies. These may have been part of a hoard of coins buried by a wealthy French nobleman, the baron of St. Castine, who had skirmished with the English in that area some 140 years earlier. The baron had been forced to flee from a British attack, and died before he had a chance to return to America. No precise record was kept, but Grindle and his son may have found up to 2,000 coins, all dated 1690 or earlier.

The Bank of New York Hoard. Around 1856 a wooden keg holding several thousand 1787 Fugio copper cents was discovered at the Bank of New York at 44 Wall Street in Manhattan. The coins—among the first money issued by the authority of the United States—were uncirculated, most with brown toning. For many years bank officials gave them to clients as souvenirs and keepsakes. When numismatist Damon G. Douglas examined the hoard in 1948 there 1,641 coins left. The bank still holds them today.

The Nichols Find of Copper Cents. About 1,000 large cents dated 1796 and 1797, in Mint State, were distributed in the 1850s by David Nichols of Massachusetts, who reportedly passed them out at face value. By 1863 the coins—by then worth $3 to $4 apiece to collectors—were all gone. Today they would be valued between $6,000 and $60,000 each even in the lowest Mint State grades, with the highest-grade pieces worth $100,000 or more!

The Randall Hoard of Copper Cents. At some point in the mid- to late 1860s, not long after the cannons of the American Civil War were silenced, a wooden keg of vintage copper large cents was brought to light. The coins—nearly bright as new—were said to have been found underneath an old railroad platform in Georgia. Inside the keg were thousands of Liberty Head cents dated between 1816 and 1820. Today most known Mint State large cents dated 1818 and 1820 in particular can be traced back to the Randall hoard—named after John Randall, a Norwich, New York, coin collector who bought most of the cents in bulk for less than their face value. Today the coins would be worth at least $500 to $1,000 each, even in the lowest Mint State grades.

The Hoard of Miser Aaron White. Aaron White was an attorney in mid-1800s Connecticut. Having lived through the Hard Times of the 1830s, and worried that the Civil War would bankrupt the nation, he didn't trust paper money and much preferred *coins*—so much that he hoarded more than 100,000 of them. His accumulation is said to have included 250 colonial and state copper coins; 60,000 copper large cents; 60,000 copper-nickel Flying Eagle and Indian Head cents (most dated 1862 and 1863); 5,000 two-cent pieces; 200 half dollars; 100 silver dollars; 350 gold dollars; and 20,000 to 30,000 foreign copper coins.

The Baltimore Find of 1934. On August 31, 1934, two boys were playing in the cellar of a rented house at 132 South Eden Street, Baltimore, when they made a startling discovery: a hoard of treasure, hidden in a wall! The Baltimore Find was more than 3,558 gold coins, all dated before 1857, including many choice and gem Mint State examples. A courtroom drama unfolded as various people staked their claims to the fortune. The following May many of the coins were auctioned; by then, some had already been quietly sold off. The story of this famous hoard is told in *Treasure in the Cellar: A Tale of Gold in Depression-Era Baltimore,* by Leonard Augsburger.

The Redfield Hoard of Silver Dollars. Lavere Redfield was an eccentric who didn't trust the government and refused to pay taxes. He moved to Reno, Nevada, in the 1930s with money he'd made in investments, and went around town looking like a poor farmer or junkman even while he was gambling thousands of dollars at the local casinos. During this time Redfield started hoarding silver dollars, buying them in bags from local banks whenever he could. He paid for the coins in cash, hauled them home in his pickup truck, and dumped them by the bagful down a coal chute to his cellar. When Redfield passed away in 1974, his hidden treasure was discovered: a quantity somewhere north of 520,000 silver dollars.

The New Orleans Bank Find of 1982. On October 29, 1982, at a few minutes past noon, a bulldozer in New Orleans broke open a treasure trove of long-hidden silver coins, believed to have been stored in three wooden boxes in the early 1840s. Soon businessmen in suits, ladies in dresses, and other passersby were scrambling in the mud to dig up some of the treasure. There were mostly Spanish colonial pieces, but also hundreds of U.S. coins, including 1840 and 1841 Liberty Seated quarters produced at the New Orleans Mint. Speculation is that the coins were a secret reserve of some long-forgotten business or bank.

The Wreck of the *Central America*. On September 12, 1857, the steamship SS *Central America*, heading from Havana, Cuba, to New York City, was swamped by a monster hurricane. The ship was carrying about $2,600,000 in gold treasure, all of which went to the bottom of the sea along with Captain William Lewis Herndon (last seen standing on the paddle box) and some 435 other passengers and crew. In 1987 the wreck was found—7,200 feet below the surface. Over time more than $100 million worth of gold coins and ingots (some weighing up to 80 pounds) were brought up from the depths.

The Wreck of the *Brother Jonathan*. In the 1990s another sidewheel steamer was found: the SS *Brother Jonathan*, lost with few survivors on January 30, 1865, as she attempted to return to harbor in Crescent City, California, after hitting stormy weather on her way north to Oregon. More than 1,000 gold coins were recovered, including many Mint State 1865 double eagles minted in San Francisco.

The Wells Fargo Hoard of 1908 Double Eagles. Coin dealer Ron Gillio purchased a hoard of 19,900 examples of the 1908 No Motto $20 gold piece in the 1990s. For a time these were stored in a Wells Fargo Bank branch, giving the cache its popular nickname. All of the coins were in Mint State—and many in choice and gem quality. They were sold off over a period of several years.

The Midwest Hoard of 1998. The single largest hoard of U.S. coins—15,290 pounds of cents and nickels from the 1800s and early 1900s—was found hidden in the walls of a Midwestern coin collector's house in 1998. The accumulation, gathered over the course of 25 years in canvas bags and 55-gallon drums, caused the floorboards to sag under its massive weight. Littleton Coin Company bought the hoard of 950,000 Indian Head cents, 308,000 Liberty Head nickels, and 488,000 Buffalo nickels, and it took several months to ship the coins to its New Hampshire headquarters.

The Big Sky Hoard of Eisenhower Dollars. In 2011 a remarkable hoard of Eisenhower dollars—more than 220,000 of them!—was found in a Montana bank vault, where they'd sat for 30 years, stored away by a prominent Montana family. Most of the coins were still in their original mint-sewn bags. They'd been shipped from the Denver Mint directly to a Federal Reserve Bank in Montana, and never saw circulation.